McGraw-Hill's

CAREERS FOR

ANIMAL LOVERS

& Other Zoological Types

Careers for You Series

McGraw-Hill's

CAREERS FOR

ANIMAL LOVERS

& Other Zoological Types

LOUISE MILLER

THIRD EDITION

New York Chicago San Francisco Lisbon London Madrid Mexico City
Milan New Delhi San Juan Seoul Singapore Sydney Toronto

The *McGraw·Hill* Companies

Library of Congress Cataloging-in-Publication Data

Miller, Louise.
    Careers for animal lovers & other zoological types / by Louise Miller — 3rd ed.
        p.   cm. — (McGraw-Hill careers for you series)
        ISBN 0-07-147615-6 (alk. paper)
        1. Animal specialists—Vocational guidance.   2. Animal culture—Vocational
guidance. I. Title. II. Title: Careers for animal lovers and other zoological
types.

SF80.M55 2007
636.0023—dc22   2006028910

1 2 3 4 5 6 7 8 9 10 11 12 13 14 15   DOC/DOC   0 9 8 7

ISBN-13: 978-0-07-147615-7
ISBN-10:   0-07-147615-6

McGraw-Hill books are available at special quantity discounts to use as premiums and
sales promotions, or for use in corporate training programs. For more information,
please write to the Director of Special Sales, Professional Publishing, McGraw-Hill,
Two Penn Plaza, New York, NY 10121-2298. Or contact your local bookstore.

This book is printed on acid-free paper.

This book is lovingly dedicated to Susie, Eloise, Natty Bumppo, Mugwump, Baby, and Buster—from whom I learned all the most important lessons in life.

Contents

Acknowledgments

The author gratefully acknowledges the following individuals for their contributions:

Kay Alport	Dog and Cat Portraiture
John Caruso	Humane Education Director
Kathleen Deering, D.V.M.	Veterinarian
Allen Feldman	Aquarist
Dori Ganan and	4Legs Pet Supply and
Leslie Corral	Adoptions Resource Center
Sara Meghrouni	Outreach Coordinator,
	Save-the-Dolphins Project
Nicholas J. Millman	Research Assistant
Patti Moran	Pet Sitters International
Jim Morgan	Morgan's Dogs
George Ney	Cat House Originals
Lauren Passen	Veterinary Technician
Elizabeth Schmitt	Technical Consultant

Foreword

I n the decade since this book was first published, many things about the world of animal careers have changed dramatically while some have not. What has changed is that, in addition to the traditional opportunities that existed, new and specialized occupations have taken their places alongside the familiar ones. What remains constant is the great need for compassionate and caring individuals to dedicate themselves to the betterment of the treatment and living conditions of animals, both wild and domesticated.

Computer software and Internet applications in the field are rapidly multiplying. Animal behavior management has moved from the fringe to the forefront of rehabilitation efforts in many shelters. Humane education continues to take center stage, recognizing the need for prevention and cure—no longer satisfied with simply managing the problem.

Because my career centers around animal welfare, I am more familiar with advances in that area, but it is true that similar trends are underway in the disciplines that concern themselves with habitat and wildlife preservation. Society at large is changing and has begun to accept that the treatment of animals, both wild and domesticated, is a barometer of the health of a civilized and compassionate culture. The movement is far from complete, but we have recently seen the wholesale embrace, by mental health professionals and social workers, of truths that we have long suspected in animal welfare—that everything from indifference to human misery to outright violence is at least partly rooted in a desensitization process that often begins with animal cruelty and neglect.

In today's hectic world, it is too easy to lose sight of the fact that animals are marvels and that in healing and protecting them we learn how to do the same for ourselves. When we can make our living in pursuit of these goals, many of us find the formula for true happiness.

While many animal careers require specific education and experience, all careers in this field need committed individuals to bring the skills and knowledge that they already have and apply them in jobs that are intellectually satisfying and emotionally rewarding. I started as a volunteer in an animal shelter and found a calling that I had not foreseen. A degree in anthropology and an overwhelming desire to make a difference was all that I brought to the table. I wanted to make a difference in the world, and, as a result, I have made a profound change in the course and quality of my life.

David Dinger
Vice President of Operations
Anti-Cruelty Society
Chicago, Illinois

CHAPTER ONE

Finding the Career That's Right for You

A nimals and people have much in common. We all need food, a place we can call home, a family and social life, training to enable us to survive in our habitat, health care, and protection. Animals, like people, come in all shapes and sizes, and their needs are met in different ways. Like humans, animal parents care for their young until they are ready to take care of themselves. Domestic animals and those in zoos or aquariums have some of these needs taken care of by humans.

Because there is such a wide variety of animals, there is a wide variety of possible careers—some deal directly with the animals, some involve animal shelters or protective agencies, and some are considered creative. Some careers involve jobs in business, while other careers are concerned with conservation of habitats and species.

How Do You Know if You're an Animal Lover?

And how do you know whether you would like to devote your working life to animals? There may be some signs in the patterns of your life that could be clear indications. At the top of the list might be whether you are the one in your family who brings home stray cats or dogs to take care of, even on a temporary basis. Or maybe you'd rather go to the zoo or aquarium than go to a movie or a ball game. If your bookshelf is filled with books about pandas or bears or lions, that might also be a sign. If you love long nature walks in the woods and bring your camera along to take pictures of the birds and other animals, you might have found your career without even looking for it.

These indications don't always come at an early age. Sometimes a person is gainfully employed as an insurance agent and gets her first dog at age twenty-five or thirty. Then she spends all her spare time with the dog, finds friends who are dog owners, and suddenly knows that fate has provided her with a new path in life—to become a dog trainer.

Let's Take a Little Test

If any of the habits described above sound like you, then you might want to answer the following questions, which will help you focus on the type of career that may suit you best:

1. Do I genuinely care about the welfare of animals?
2. Am I willing to work long hours doing stressful work?
3. Will I be happy living on a modest income?
4. Am I willing to spend several years on education and training?
5. Can I show empathy with people in times of grief?
6. Do I have physical and mental strength and energy?
7. Can I exercise good judgment and solve problems under difficult circumstances?
8. Am I reliable and compassionate?
9. Do I have up-to-date computer, organizational, and communication skills?
10. Am I willing to relocate to areas where jobs are available?

If you answered yes to all or most of these questions, you are ready to look at the opportunities available to the animal lover in you.

What Kinds of Careers Are Available?

Based on the preceding questions, you will now have to assess your own preferences regarding career choices. You have to decide whether you want to deal directly with animals or be an administrator, creative person, or business owner. You have to decide whether you want to work in the public or private sector. And you have to decide how much time you are willing to devote to training and education.

Some jobs allow you to work with animals and make important decisions about their health and welfare, including life-and-death decisions. Others require you to enforce laws regarding their safety, to keep records on their vital statistics, or to ensure that they are properly nourished.

You might decide that your talents lie in painting, photographing, or writing about animals and exhibiting your creative work in a gallery or publishing articles in a magazine. Or you might create a whole new career category based on your own talents and the animal needs you identify. New technological advances are creating new career choices in all fields, so the future is wide open.

Let's take a look at some of those choices.

Veterinarians

When most people think of a medical caretaker for animals, they think of the local veterinarian. Whenever the family dog or cat gets sick or needs spaying or neutering, the person we call is the veterinarian. Veterinarians in private practice are there to help protect the health and well-being of pets and to educate the owners on proper pet care and nutrition. However, veterinarians are also found in zoos and aquariums, in the classroom, in research laboratories, in regulatory agencies, in public health facilities, in the armed forces, in scientific agencies, in disaster response teams, and in wildlife management. They can also practice in animal shelters, in horse stables, at racetracks, and on fur ranches. Some write pet advice columns for newspapers or magazines, produce informational television shows, or prepare videotapes on the care or training of animals.

Veterinary Technicians

Working alongside the veterinarians are the veterinary technicians (commonly known as vet techs), who are licensed and, depending on the regulations in the state, can perform a variety of tasks under the supervision of a veterinarian. They might prepare animals for surgery or administer anesthetics. These technicians often have degrees in biology or zoology and are the most highly skilled assistants to the veterinarian.

Animal Attendants

Animal, or kennel, attendants maintain the animals on a daily basis by feeding and watering them, cleaning their cages or stalls, and washing their food dishes. Animal attendants also watch for changes in animal behavior as possible symptoms of disease. They exercise the animals and check their environments for safety.

Protective Agency Workers

Many animal lovers go into animal work to provide shelter, to protest abuse, to educate the public about the needs and rights of animals, and to help protect endangered species. Protective agencies deal with both domesticated animals and wildlife, in cities and in rural areas. Protective agencies employ both administrative and clerical staff members and also rely heavily on volunteers.

Trainers

Trainers of both domesticated and wild animals have the skills to teach animals to obey their commands. They are employed by pet owners, police or military organizations, movie and television producers, guide dog services, zoos, circuses, aquariums, and racetracks.

Groomers

Groomers usually confine their businesses to dogs, although some groom cats, too. Grooming service includes clipping nails, cleaning ears and teeth, bathing, clipping and trimming fur, and brushing and combing. Groomers sometimes also offer pet boarding services or sell various pet supplies, such as collars, flea products, food, brushes, and combs, in their shops.

Pet Salespeople

If you want to specialize in selling house pets and pet products, you have to love small animals, including dogs, cats, hamsters, snakes, fish, and birds, and should enjoy dealing with and advising pet owners. Store owners must know something about pet behavior, nutritional needs, play needs, and habitat.

Zoo Specialists

Many career opportunities exist in zoos, including zoo director, curator, veterinarian, veterinary technician, and zoologist. Zoos also employ curators of exhibits, research, and education. Many zoos also have business managers and staff for the public relations department and gift shop, in addition to clerical workers.

Aquarium Specialists

Aquariums are generally headed by a director and often an assistant director. Most will also employ a general curator and specific curators for different collections. Veterinarians may be on the staff or be on call as needed. Aquariums also hire aquarists (aquarium zoologists) and librarians.

Creative Careers

Creative career possibilities in animal work range from pet and wildlife artist to writer, designer, and photographer. Illustrators are needed to prepare exhibits, charts, teaching aids, textbook designs, magazines, and educational programs about animals. Photographers show their own work or sell to magazines and book publishers. Other artists specialize in pet portraits or paintings of wildlife.

Writers are employed by newspapers, magazines, and book publishers. They may write for children, adults, or animal specialists. Other creative people build elaborate cat condominiums or doghouses.

Pet Sitters and Pet Walkers

Pet sitting is a fast-growing industry because so many people own pets and because traveling on business trips is increasingly common among two-income families. You can be a pet sitter full-time or part-time. As a pet sitter, you exercise dogs and feed and water all manner of house pets, including dogs, cats, birds, and fish, as well as ferrets, rabbits, hamsters, gerbils, and snakes. Many pet sitters also water plants, bring in the mail, and make security checks on the homes of the people who are away.

Pet Transporters

Some pet shop owners or kennel operators have branched out into the pet transport industry. This usually includes taxi service to and from the airport but could include trips to the veterinarian, groomer, or boarding kennel. The airport pickup and delivery service is especially helpful when the owner must arrive home after the pet. Transporters often provide a boarding service for the pet until the owner arrives home.

Ornithologists

Bird lovers can find careers in research, education, and administration. Professional ornithologists work in universities and colleges, in state or federal agencies, in museums, and in conservation and consulting organizations.

Conservation and Wildlife Managers

Both state and federal agencies employ workers in wildlife research, biology, population monitoring and management, and habitat management, or as fish and game wardens and interpreters. Private associations and nonprofit agencies dealing with wildlife employ directors, legal counsel, corporate planning officers, financial officers, training directors, fund-raisers, and membership and publications directors.

Workers in the Department of the Interior

Jobs for animal lovers with the federal government are limited, but opportunities exist for biological science professionals and wildlife refuge managers. Others can work in interpretive or educational programs or as special wildlife agents to investigate and enforce fish and wildlife laws.

Various administrative and clerical positions, as well as jobs for special program workers, are available through the U.S. Fish and Wildlife Service. Some fishing and wildlife technicians are also employed, as well as equipment operators, craftspeople, and maintenance technicians.

Animal-Related Business Owners

In addition to being a pet shop owner, breeder, product salesperson, or feed supplier, other opportunities for businesses related to animals offer seemingly endless possibilities. They range from leading safaris in Africa to selling gourmet pet foods, from running pet insurance companies to managing pet cemeteries, from practicing cat astrology to renting guard dogs that jog with clients in the park.

Depending on your business experience or inclination, market needs, and changes in popular tastes, you can create your own career track. Only your imagination (and perhaps a few local ordinances) will limit you in your pursuit of the perfect career.

Responsibilities and Qualifications

Because there is such a wide range of possibilities in animal-related careers, qualifications, salaries, benefits, and responsibilities vary according to the job, location, and whether the job is with a corporation or nonprofit organization. Some jobs with animals are strictly administrative, such as the director of an animal shelter, and are involved only in the broadest way with animal caretaking. On the other hand, veterinarians, technicians, attendants, and trainers work directly with animals. Some careers require a high degree of education and training, while others require little or no previous experience in the field.

Getting Started

It is always a good idea for anyone considering animal work—whatever your age, education, or experience—to volunteer or work part-time at an animal shelter, horse stable, boarding facility, or wildlife facility before you make your final decision about educational pursuits. Or you may want to work on a farm or ranch during your summer break from school or on your vacation—just to get a feel for the job.

Many facilities will be glad to open their doors to you for guided tours, informational interviews, or videotape presentations on careers in their fields. They may have publications, such as pamphlets or brochures, for distribution to the public. Public libraries and bookstores also have specialized books, pamphlets, and videotapes available to you for study. These include the *Encyclopedia of Associations* and the *Occupational Outlook Handbook* (also online at www.bls.gov/oco). A reference librarian will point you in the right direction. Salaries for some of these careers can be found at www.salary.com or www.monster.com.

Magazines specializing in cats, dogs, horses, fish, birds, and wildlife can be found at public libraries, bookstores, and newsstands. Some specialize in care and training; others, in painting or photography of animals.

Dog trainers, boarding facility operators, and breeders may hire part-time help during their busy seasons. You should apply for these jobs—or even volunteer for a while—to see if you are really suited to a lifetime career in the field.

Your local telephone directory and professional organizations can provide you with names and addresses of people to contact for specific information on education, training, and qualifications required for individual areas of expertise and general information on salaries. Advertisements in animal-related publications supply names and addresses of schools and training facilities that can help you launch your career. Make sure that the facility at which you get your training is accredited or approved by the national professional association in the field.

Another way to get information on careers, training, and experience is to use the wide-open resources of the Internet. If you don't have a computer at home, most public libraries or your local school may provide public Internet access. When searching on websites like Google or Yahoo, just type in key words, such as *careers for zoologists*, or, if you are looking for a particular organization or association, *U.S. Fish and Wildlife Service*. You can also ask a question, such as "What is a zoologist?" Then press "search," and a world of information will open up to you. You can also find out about current books, videos, and CDs regarding animal work on the Internet.

Be aware that all of the jobs listed in this book probably require a certain degree of computer literacy, such as word processing or database software or using the Internet. So be sure to include computer training in your high school and college course work, including basic word processing, database, and spreadsheet skills.

After you have completed all your training and education, you might also find the job you want on the many career search websites, such as www.monster.com and www.jobsearch.org. Use the technology available to you, as well as the more traditional sources, to find the perfect match for you.

Now it's up to you. You began with the basic characteristic of loving animals, and now it's time to learn more about your career options. To make sure of your direction, let's take a look at some more specific questions about your attitudes that can help you make up your mind about a possible career with animals.

1. I definitely want to work directly with animals.
2. I am willing to devote several more years to my education so that I can become a highly skilled professional.
3. I prefer to work with:
   a. cats, dogs, and small pets
   b. horses
   c. wild animals
   d. farm animals
4. I prefer a steady office job with standard benefits.
5. I want to help enforce the laws concerning animal welfare.
6. I do my best work when I'm managing other people and seeing that things run smoothly.
7. I have excellent clerical skills, including knowledge of computer programs, filing, answering telephone calls, and dealing with the public.
8. I have always been able to make animals listen to me and do what I tell them.
9. I have a very good business head and have entrepreneurial inclinations.
10. I want to write about animals with other creative people, such as artists, designers, photographers, and illustrators.

Let your answers to these questions guide you as you explore some of the careers available in animal work. There is, truly, something for everyone!

For More Information

Alessandrini, Jodi, and Kathy Kinser. *Puppy Stuff: A Concise, Informational Baby Book for Today's Busy Puppy "Parents."* Pallachip Publishing, 1997.

Dwelle, Jacqueline. *Your First Horse: How to Buy and Care for Your First Horse.* Hoofbeat Publications, 1998.

Marinelli, Deborah A. *Careers in Animal Care and Veterinary Science.* Rosen Publishing Group, 2001.

Murphy, Jana. *The Secret Lives of Dogs: The Real Reasons Behind 52 Mysterious Canine Behaviors.* Rodale Books, 2000.

Nemec, Gale B. *Living with Cats.* Diane Books Publishing Company, 1997.

Pavia, Audrey. *Careers with Animals.* Barron's Educational Series, 2001.

Solisti-Matteson, Kate, and Patrice Mattelon. *The Holistic Animal Handbook: A Guidebook to Nutrition, Health, and Communication.* Council Oaks Books, 2004.

U.S. Department of Labor. *Occupational Outlook Handbook.* McGraw-Hill, annual.

Viner, Bradley. *The Cat Owner's Question & Answer Book.* Barron's Educational Series, Inc., 1998.

CHAPTER TWO

Ensuring Animals' Good Health

A nyone who has ever had a pet has probably encountered a vet. When Fido was sick, or Gabby needed shots, or Princess needed to be spayed, we loaded our terrified friend into the car for a trip to the local animal hospital. Maybe even then we thought about becoming a veterinarian because we thought it would be wonderful to heal and comfort our animal companions.

Veterinarians

If you look into what it takes to become a veterinarian and what veterinarians actually do, you might be surprised. You probably know that veterinarians diagnose and treat sick and injured animals, but you may not know just how much education is required to earn a doctor of veterinary medicine (D.V.M.) degree.

Education Requirements

Currently, a doctor of veterinary medicine degree can be earned at twenty-eight accredited universities in the United States and four in Canada. Although career opportunities abound for veterinarians, only about 35 percent of all applicants are accepted to veterinary programs.

A very useful publication for anyone interested in becoming a veterinarian is the annual *Veterinary Medical School Admission Requirements in the United States and Canada*. This publication can help you prepare for admission. Each of the thirty-two accredited universities in the United States and Canada provides information that you will need regarding prerequisites, special programs, and deadlines. The publication also explains the many career opportunities available to veterinarians, such as community health, food resource management, space biology, and wildlife conservation, as well as the more traditional veterinary medicine practices.

The veterinary colleges in Canada are located in Quebec, Ontario, Saskatchewan, and Prince Edward Island. According to the Canadian Veterinary Medical Association, 75 percent of Canadian vets work in private practices caring for small or large animals or for specific species. Another 10 percent work for the government, and the remaining 15 percent are teachers or researchers or work in various capacities in private industry.

To receive a D.V.M. in Canada, you must take two years of pre-veterinary courses at a university and four years (five in Quebec) at one of the four veterinary colleges, which only graduate about four hundred veterinarians every year.

In both Canada and the United States, it is wise to take basic science courses in high school, such as biology, chemistry, and physics. Actually working with animals as a volunteer in an animal shelter, clinic, or laboratory during school breaks or after school helps you know whether you want to work with animals and would weigh in your favor when applying for admittance to a veterinary program.

Just to qualify for admission to a U.S. college of veterinary medicine, you must have earned a bachelor's degree, preferably in one of the biological sciences. Core courses in college should include chemistry, physics, biochemistry, animal biology, zoology, and physiology. You should also have a solid background in language skills, mathematics, and the humanities. However, since each of the veterinary colleges has different admission requirements, you should check the school of your choice and take the undergraduate courses required for that particular program.

As a student of veterinary medicine, you may have a choice of curricula, depending on the school you choose. This is largely as a result of the changing nature of pet owners, who are becoming more and more sophisticated in their demands to keep the quality of the lives of their dogs and cats at a very high level for as long as possible. This has created a demand for nontraditional animal health care, including such specialties as animal dentistry and hip-replacement surgery, which means there is a growing need for such specialists.

Veterinary colleges may gear their courses exclusively toward these more specialized career paths. Some schools provide a more generalized curriculum dealing with all species. Others have created specialized tracks that the student picks in the second year. Still others combine the two approaches, devoting the first two years to core courses, then providing a variety of electives in the third year and a specialized track in the fourth year.

Core courses generally include anatomy, physiology, pathology, pharmacology, and microbiology. At this stage, your education is mostly theoretical, although there would likely be some laboratory work. Later, your course work is involved more with clinical and surgical training, working directly with animals and their owners.

As might be expected, the emphasis in this stage may be on applied anatomy, diseases, obstetrics, and radiology. Public health, preventive medicine, and nutrition are dealt with at this point in your education, as well as professional ethics and business practices.

After graduating from a veterinary program with a D.V.M. degree, you will still be required to get a state license before going into practice. Most states and Canadian provinces also require that you pass an exam about that state's laws and regulations.

Throughout their careers, veterinarians must also keep up with every new scientific discovery and technological advance.

Career Paths for Veterinarians

The great majority of veterinarians in the United States work in private practice, and most of them work only on small animals, usually cats and dogs. A much smaller number work with larger animals, such as horses or farm animals; some generalists work with both pets and livestock. All told, veterinarians look after the health of literally millions of animals per year.

Of the veterinarians who do not go into private practice, some become researchers or teachers. Others may find careers with state or federal agencies as regulatory agents, inspectors, disease control specialists, animal control workers, epidemiologists, or environmental workers. Still others work at zoos, aquariums, and animal shelters.

Veterinarians who choose to educate the next generation of veterinarians are also encouraged to publish articles in professional journals and are involved in helping practicing veterinarians continue their educations by teaching new techniques and methods.

Veterinarians who specialize in research can be found not only at universities but also in private industry and government agencies. These veterinarians seek new ways to prevent health problems in animals, and in the process they sometimes discover new ways to treat humans, too.

Veterinarians who choose to go into regulatory work are charged with the responsibility of controlling livestock diseases and making sure that those diseases do not affect the public. Those who work for the U.S. Department of Agriculture or state or local government agencies also have to inspect and sometimes quarantine animals that are brought into the country or across state lines.

Veterinarians in public health work for federal, state, or local governments, which affords them a wide variety of positions. As epidemiologists, they investigate outbreaks of diseases. Others work in the larger realm of the environment, where they check water supplies or food processing plants for safety. They may also study the impact of pesticides and pollutants on the environment or be called in to respond to emergency rescue of animals as a result of natural or human-caused disasters. In the laboratory, veterinarians work on immunization and quarantine programs.

As a veterinarian in the military services, you would probably be in the U.S. Army Veterinary Corps, a branch of the Army Medical Department. Army veterinarians are engaged in animal disease prevention, laboratory animal medicine, pathology, food hygiene, and preventive medicine. They also provide regular veterinary services to government-owned animals and treat pets of members of the armed services wherever they are stationed in the world.

The private sector employs veterinarians in research and development in such fields as pharmacology, parasitology, microbiology, and endocrinology, primarily for new product development. Some veterinarians work their way up to positions in production and quality control, marketing, sales, or even management. Companies in the food industry, agribusiness, and pharmaceuticals also are possibilities for employment.

Basically, wherever animals are, there also are veterinarians—in neighborhood animal hospitals, in animal shelters, in zoos and aquariums, at racetracks, and in wildlife management facilities. No matter where they work, veterinarians must like and respect animals and also be able to work well with people, very often under stressful circumstances.

Making a Living as a Veterinarian

Depending on your choice of veterinary work, your working conditions will vary. In private practice, universities, laboratories, and offices, you will generally work regular hours with a steady income and good benefits. However, if you work with livestock or horses, you may be working outdoors in all kinds of weather. Hours can be long and irregular, and the work can be hazardous.

Although veterinarians' incomes also vary according to background, experience, and specialization, as a new graduate you can expect to start at about $29,900 per year after graduation, with the average annual income of a veterinarian in private practice at $57,500. The future prospects for employment as a veterinarian seem to be quite good, especially for those with training in specialties such as cardiology, dentistry, acupuncture, and hip-replacement surgery.

A Veterinarian at Work

Kathleen Deering is a veterinarian who, early in her life, was introduced through her father and grandfather to the wonder of the human-animal bond. They nurtured injured wildlife and took in stray companions or exotic animals and tended lovingly to an aquarium and a variety of finches. On summer vacations, her father fostered in Kathleen new fascinations with amphibians, reptiles, fish, and larger woodland creatures. Later vacations included trips to Gatorland, Sea World, and wild animal parks. And her mother took her and her siblings on regular visits to the zoo, which Kathleen always found fascinating.

Kathleen also had a knack for having multitudes of stray dogs and cats find her and "follow" her home. Her family served as foster parents until they could reunite lost animals with their families or place them into adoptive homes. Her fierce love of animals extended, of course, to their several family pets.

By the time she got to high school, Kathleen knew that she wanted to help animals in some way but was somewhat discouraged about pursuing a career in veterinary medicine because of the highly competitive nature of being accepted into such a program. Somewhat later, though, she met a fellow student who became a study partner in their science classes. He was a technician at an animal hospital who was preparing to apply for a veterinary college. His encouragement was all she needed to help her make up her mind to pursue veterinary medicine, and she was able to take his place at the hospital when he left for college. There she gained experience as an animal, surgical, and laboratory technician and attendant while she earned her bachelor and master of science degrees and until she was accepted into veterinary school.

Kathleen has some concrete educational advice for people who wish to become veterinarians. In high school, master the core sciences, such as biology, inorganic and organic chemistry, physics, and microbiology, as well as math, history, and English. Computer skills are necessary for literature searches and research and are essential for some specialty areas, such as epidemiology or public health. Business management courses are helpful for those who want to open a private practice.

In order to get into a veterinary school, you should have some experience working with both large and small animals, especially in a veterinary practice setting. It's important to keep a journal of your experiences while preparing to apply for admission. Those notes will help you thoroughly document your background to the admissions committee. And your academic record, needless to say, has to be very strong because of the fierce competition.

After you have completed four years of course work—laboratory, surgical, and clinical training in an accredited college of veterinary medicine—you must pass the computer-based North American Veterinary Licensing Examination and pass the state board exams. Then you can start your career as a veterinarian.

Kathleen thinks that you have to like and work well with people as much as you do animals when you practice veterinary medicine. Compassion, empathy, patience, and the ability to work under stressful and physically and emotionally demanding conditions are also very important. She truly enjoys the many ways the companion animals enrich their guardians' lives and those of others fortunate enough to be touched by them. She feels blessed to have the talents and tools necessary to maintain those cherished bonds for as long as possible. Kathleen feels that few experiences in our lifetimes grant us the rewards that such unconditional and enriching relationships provide. She recommends that you follow your heart if you want to get into this rewarding and respected career. Know what you are getting into and be certain about your commitment. Few professions offer the versatility a veterinary medicine degree affords, and training institutions can guide you about the many different paths that are available to you today.

Veterinary Technicians

Veterinary technicians work alongside the veterinarian. This is a comparatively new position in animal care. Because of increased demands on the veterinarian, more and more animals are benefiting from the specialized training of the technician. Although duties may vary from practice to practice, the primary responsibilities of a veterinary technician usually include administering and monitoring anesthesia, assisting with imaging techniques, taking blood counts, and preparing tissue samples. All of this work is done under the direct supervision of the veterinarian, scientist, or senior technician.

Education Requirements

In the middle of the twentieth century, most veterinarians provided on-the-job training for their assistants. But veterinary work became so much more sophisticated and technically advanced that formal academic training became popular in the 1960s. Now more than seventy college programs are accredited by the American Veterinary Medical Association. These usually include two years of study leading to an associate's degree in applied science. Some schools offer four-year degree programs.

You can begin preparing for a career in veterinary technology early. Most veterinary technician programs require a high school diploma or its equivalent and often successful completion of specific courses in high school. Therefore, you may want to talk to your career counselor for help in finding the admission requirements for the programs that suit you best. Most require a strong background in science in either high school or college.

Required course work in veterinary technician programs usually includes chemistry, mathematics, humanities, communication skills, and biology. In addition, more specialized course work might include physiology, anatomy, biochemistry, nutrition, and parasitology. Many accredited schools suggest that you use the summer break for obtaining practical job-related experience at a clinic or animal shelter. In addition to the U.S. programs accredited by the American Veterinary Medical Association, ten colleges and technical institutes in Canada offer vet tech programs.

After you receive your degree as a veterinary technician, you may have to become registered or certified by the state or province in which you will practice, and registration requirements vary. The American Veterinary Medical Association provides a synopsis of these regulations for practicing in the United States.

Once you are on the job, in addition to the required technical skills, you need a large dose of patience, empathy, and understanding as you treat sick and injured animals and deal with their owners, who are also under stress. The scope of your responsibilities will depend on the veterinarian you work for and the type of facility where you work. These facilities include clinics, animal shelters, zoos, horse farms, racetracks, kennels, research and diagnostic laboratories, pharmaceutical companies, and schools.

Making a Living as a Veterinary Technician

Job opportunities abound for vet techs in a variety of settings. Depending on where you work, job responsibilities include giving medicine, applying bandages, managing nutritional programs, taking patient histories, collecting specimens, preparing patients for surgery or radiation, and assisting in research projects.

Professional associations make it possible for veterinary technicians to continue their education and to network with others in the field, either at social events or in professional settings. The national professional organization in this field is the North American Veterinary Technician Association, but the American Veterinary Medical Association also provides lists of local and state organizations for veterinary technicians.

A Practicing Veterinary Technician

Lauren Passen is a veterinary technician who grew up with animals—from lizards, dogs, fish, and mice to a guinea pig, baby chicken, snake, and tarantula. The earliest pet she remembers was her rabbit, Sammy, but she also loved the giraffes at the zoo.

Lauren knew she loved both animals and science, so in college, Lauren took as many science courses as she could. She discovered primatology, putting her on the track of becoming a primatologist. She volunteered at the local zoo, where she worked with the orangutans. However, at that time, Lauren decided that she did not want to be traveling her whole life and chose to become a veterinary technician.

At the end of her freshman year, Lauren became involved with the local humane society and began what turned out to be a four-year volunteer experience. Since her college did not offer many specific courses directed toward the veterinary field, she concentrated on chemistry, biology, and zoology classes.

After graduation, Lauren began a two-year program to become a vet tech, which included medical terminology, veterinary science, anatomy, microbiology, parasitology, hematology, radiology, and anesthesia—courses that were invaluable once she began working. Her last semester consisted of an internship at a clinic, where she admits to learning more than during her two years in school. Working at a clinic now with some of the smartest, most clinically intellectual people she has known, Lauren is learning every day through contact with her colleagues and personal clinical experiences.

Lauren believes that a vet tech has to be extremely patient, compassionate, emotionally and physically strong, and know how to act at the drop of a hat. Lauren has found out that a major misconception of the job is that vet techs deal with animals all day long. She knows now that people skills are extremely important in order to succeed in this line of work. Her greatest challenge is learning how to deal with euthanasia. It is never easy, and it is only done when it is in the best interest of the animal. Lauren has been told that the day euthanasia becomes easy is the day she should find a new career.

Lauren's best advice to you if you are thinking of joining the veterinary field is to make sure that this is what you really love, volunteer as often as possible, and join a professional organization. This is not a career to get into if you are looking to make a lot of money or have a lot of free time. The pay is minimal, and the hours are long. But the look in an animal's eyes after it has been nursed back to health is indescribable and by far Lauren's greatest reward.

Animal Caretakers

If you have a real commitment to the everyday care, feeding, and cleaning of animals, you may choose to become a full- or part-time animal attendant or caretaker. Grooming and exercising animals are included in this job, as well as cleaning cages. These duties are performed in animal shelters and hospitals, boarding or breeding kennels, stables, grooming shops, zoos, and aquariums.

You might even work with an ambulance crew or as an overnight animal shelter caretaker. You may be called on to keep basic records and, in some cases, to do some manual labor, such as basic carpentry, painting, lawn maintenance, or digging graves for deceased animals.

If you are looking for a glamour job in animal work, this one is probably not for you. As an attendant, your work involves hard, often dirty, often repetitive, but absolutely necessary work.

Working closely with the animals, you get to know their personalities, temperaments, and needs firsthand. Your rewards are largely intangible, but you have the joy of experiencing the positive responses of a recovering or lonely animal as it is emotionally or physically healing from injury or disease.

Jobs for Animal Caretakers

Working as an animal caretaker in a stable means that you would be responsible for cleaning out barns or stalls, feeding the horses, brushing them, cleaning their hooves, and trimming their manes and tails. Then you may have to harness and saddle the horses, exercise them, rub them down, and cool them down after a ride.

Horse caretakers or attendants also clean the tack room and polish the saddles. Feed bags and other supplies for the stable may be heavy, but you may be called on to unload them when they are delivered.

In an animal shelter, either private or public, your responsibilities as an animal attendant would be different from those in the stable. Basic cleaning, grooming, and feeding are the same. At an animal shelter, however, you may also keep records and screen potential adopters. Sometimes shelter attendants or caretakers also serve as animal control officers who pick up stray animals and rescue animals that are trapped or otherwise impaired. Attendants may also field calls concerning potential abuse or cruelty toward animals. Many animal shelters now ask animal attendants to serve as adoption counselors for people who have never owned a pet. Since they know the adoptive pets so well, they are able to match them up with their new owners.

In a veterinary hospital or clinic, animal attendants are called veterinary assistants. They perform the basic daily duties for the well-being of the animals. In addition, they may help prepare equipment and instruments for surgery or help hold the animals while they are being treated by the veterinarian. All instructions given by the veterinarian regarding diet and care of the sick or injured animal have to be followed precisely by the animal caretaker. The caretaker in a hospital may also be called on to communicate with the pets' owners and perform some clerical duties, such as answering telephones, keeping records, and making appointments.

If you work as an attendant or caretaker in a laboratory, you may have to keep records on experiments, observe effects of drugs or medication on the animals, and sterilize equipment. You may also record special diets or nutritional needs of the animals and clean cages.

You should keep in mind that some of the animals in your care may die, and for someone who has cared for an animal, death can be a traumatic experience. Before becoming an animal caretaker, you should think about whether you can deal with the realities of pain and death with animals you love.

Becoming an Animal Caretaker

Since there are no educational or training requirements for animal caretaker or attendant positions, many people come to these jobs as volunteers and work up to a staff position. Volunteering gives you the opportunity to see whether you have what it takes to be an animal caretaker. You should also think about which area you would feel most comfortable in—an animal hospital, shelter, stable, laboratory, or aquarium.

If you are still in school and are contemplating working as a caretaker, you should take English, mathematics, and social studies. Additionally, biology, chemistry, science, physiology, or psychology would be helpful. Any courses in animal behavior and business administration are a bonus.

There is a rather high turnover rate among animal caretakers, so employment opportunities are good. Also, people are demanding better care of their animals. Salaries, however, are generally poor. The work is steady, though, because animals often need round-the-clock attention, and you cannot always leave work at 5 P.M. Benefits often include paid vacation, health and life insurance, a pension plan, and sick days.

If you are already working but are thinking about changing your career to animal work, you might want to work as a volunteer at an animal hospital, boarding kennel, animal shelter, or training facility for a time to see whether this is a good fit for you. Remember that your physical strength, emotional sensitivity, ability to deal with difficult situations, patience, and thoroughness are valuable qualities to bring to any work with animals. They are especially valuable, however, for those whose jobs require daily physical contact with pets, livestock, or wildlife.

More Opportunities for Animal Caregivers

Here are several more career options for animal lovers who want to be part of ensuring animals' good health.

Pet Therapists

Companion animals are becoming more popular with people who live in small city apartments; they no longer belong only to suburban families with backyards or wide open spaces. With the demands and dangers of city life and with more owners working outside the home for longer hours, pets may need special help to cope with the anxieties associated with new experiences.

Cats are currently considered the most popular companion animal, partially because they are more self-sufficient than dogs. They are perfect pets for working people, apartment dwellers, and single people. As the number of cat owners continues to grow, so, probably, will the need for pet therapists.

You must have a genuine concern and sensitivity for animals if you want to enter this field. A background in psychology or animal behavior would be extremely helpful. As the field expands, training in animal husbandry, wildlife management, and biology may also be required.

The pioneering work being done by pet therapists now may also serve as the basis for further research and treatment for farm and other animals. Your imagination and creativity in this new field may come into play, as well as your technical skills and empathy and compassion.

Zoos and Aquariums

Animals in zoos and aquariums also need proper nutrition, a compatible habitat, and proper medical attention. Because of the size of these facilities and of the animals themselves, many caretakers are needed for their welfare—veterinarians, attendants, technicians, nutritionists, and biologists.

Since the natural habitats of these animals have been destroyed in many parts of the world, one of the main functions of zoos, aquariums, and wildlife management facilities is to provide the animals with the kind of environment and food that is conducive to their health and well-being, as well as their propagation. Having wild animals in captivity provides humans with an otherwise unavailable look at other species, which should lead to understanding and respect.

Veterinarians as Teachers

Colleges and universities specializing in veterinary medicine rely on other veterinarians to teach, publish, consult, and perform research. An ability to transmit ideas and to evaluate student progress is needed in this career, in addition to a thorough knowledge of veterinary medicine. Without teachers to guide the next generation of caretakers, whole generations of animals might be lost due to injury, neglect, disease, and overpopulation.

Preserving Animal Health in Other Ways

Without veterinarians in regulatory work, diseases could spread rapidly from animals to humans, especially if the animals have come into the country from other parts of the world. So the veterinarian in regulatory work is very much concerned with the health and well-being of humans, if only indirectly.

Of course, diseases are more often transmitted from animal to animal, and that's why animal epidemiologists are important. Tracing the origin of the disease and finding a cure will help preserve the species involved, as well as the lives of the afflicted animals.

Pollution affects both humans and animals in many ways every day. Water and air quality are crucial to sustain all forms of life, as well as to ensure future generations. Pesticides affect the food chain for all land creatures, and sea animals are just as affected by oil spills as we are. Veterinarians who specialize in environmental hazards for animals will again indirectly aid human preservation.

Animals used for sport, such as racehorses, need excellent daily care and nutrition if they are to perform to their full potential. Many caretakers are necessary to maintain these sleek animals' well-being. And when they take off from the starting gate, it's easy to see why they are so cherished.

Animal Care Is Important to Everyone

You might ask yourself why there is such a wide range of work available for those who choose to be animal caretakers. From the most highly skilled professional—the veterinarian—to the dog or cat kennel attendant, animal caretakers play a vital role in the life of our society. Healthy, loving companion animals bring a great deal of joy to their human owners and provide lifelong companionship. They have been known to help sick people get better and older people feel young again. Having a pet in your life is a privilege and offers all of us a daily glimpse into the life and behavior of another species.

Those who take care of animals, then, are necessary to preserve the health of individual animals as well as that of the species. Indi-

rectly, they also support the welfare of humans by helping to preserve the vital ecological balance between and among the many
species on the planet.

Now you know which caretaker careers are available and how to
prepare for them. You also know why these careers are so important to the physical and emotional welfare of animals and, indirectly, of humans. And you may know a bit more about where you
would be working as a caretaker.

The next step is to do a little more research to be sure that
you're on the right track. Volunteer at your local animal shelter or
clinic. Contact your local animal hospital and see if a veterinarian
or veterinary technician will talk to you about the job. Or maybe
you could work part-time as an animal attendant. You can read
every article there is on pet therapy or specialized books from
your community library. Check the Internet for animal-related
websites. Don't be afraid to plunge in and ask, read, and research.
There is a lot of work to be done, and caretakers are usually willing to talk about their work. They are, after all, hard-working professionals who are proud of their work and want to share
information with interested people. And remember—the sooner
you start, the sooner you'll be working with the animals you love!

For More Information

Publications

Bowman-Kruhm, Mary. *A Day in the Life of a Veterinarian.*
PowerKids Press, 1999.

Gustafson, R.W. *Room to Roam: More Tales of a Montana
Veterinarian.* Two Dot Books, 1996.

Lee, Mary Price, with Richard S. Lee. *Opportunities in Animal
and Pet Care Careers.* McGraw-Hill, 2001.

Marinelli, Deborah A. *Careers in Animal Care and Veterinary
Science.* Rosen Publishing Group, 2000.

Sawicki, Stephen. *Animal Hospital.* Chicago Review Press, 1997.

Schaefer, Lola M. *We Need Veterinarians.* Capstone Press, 2006.

Slim, Ray. *Animal Rescue in Flood and Swiftwater Incidents.* CFS Press, 1999.

Smith, Carin A. *Career Choices for Veterinarians: Beyond Private Practice.* Smith Veterinary Services, 1998.

Swope, Robert E., Julie Rigby, and Leonard F. Seda. *Opportunities in Veterinary Medicine Careers.* McGraw-Hill, 2001.

Wright, John C., and Judi Wright Lashnits. *The Dog Who Would Be King: Tales and Surprising Lessons from a Pet Psychologist.* Rodale Books, 1999.

Wright, John C., and Judi Wright Lashnits. *Is Your Cat Crazy? Solutions from the Casebook of a Cat Therapist.* Howell Book House, 1996.

Zucker, Martin. *The Veterinarians' Guide to Natural Remedies for Cats: Safe and Effective Alternative Treatments and Healing Techniques from the Nation's Top Holistic Veterinarians.* Three Rivers Press, 2000.

Associations

American Association for Laboratory Animal Science
9190 Crestwyn Hills Drive
Memphis, TN 38125
www.aalas.org

American Boarding Kennels Association
1702 East Pikes Peak Avenue
Colorado Springs, CO 80909
www.abka.com

American College of Veterinary Surgeons
11 North Washington Street, Suite 720
Rockville, MD 20850
www.acvs.org

American Holistic Veterinary Medical Association
2218 Old Emmerton Road
Bel Air, MD 21015
www.ahvma.org

American Veterinary Chiropractic Association
442154 East 140 Road
Bluejacket, OK 74333
www.animalchiropractic.org

American Veterinary Medical Association
1931 North Meacham Road, Suite 100
Schaumburg, IL 60173
www.avma.org

American Veterinary Society of Animal Behavior
www.avsab.us

Canadian Veterinary Medical Association
339 Booth Street
Ottawa, Ontario K1R 7K1
Canada
www.canadianveterinarians.net

National Association of Veterinary Technicians in America
PO Box 224
Battle Ground, IN 47920
www.navta.net

CHAPTER THREE

Working in Animal Shelters and Refuges

Until people are educated in the humane treatment of animals, there will be a need for animal rescue teams, rehabilitation services, and animal shelters. Many organizations are working to get the word out to schoolchildren and adults about how to live with our animal friends, both wild and domesticated. Animals are often abused, mistreated, or abandoned by those who should be taking care of them, and sometimes wild animals are injured by natural predators, traps, or motorized vehicles. Birds often fly into buildings or power lines. Other animals are victims of oil spills, environmental pollution, or land development that seriously damages or destroys their natural habitats.

Regardless of how animals arrive at the point of needing help, medical care, rehabilitation, and temporary homes are available. If it is a domesticated animal, private and public animal shelters provide care. Wildlife refuges and rehabilitation centers either provide a natural habitat for undomesticated animals or care for them until they are released back into the wild.

Working for Local Private Shelters

Local private shelters for domesticated animals (which often have the phrases "humane society" or "society for the prevention of cruelty to animals" in their names), usually house dogs and cats, but often other animals, such as pigs, chickens, and birds, are brought in. These animal shelters are generally nonprofit agencies but are organized like a business. Therefore, in addition to veterinarians, veterinary technicians, and animal caretakers, they provide careers for administrative and support staff and sometimes for investigators, lawyers, and accountants.

Private shelters in large cities can take in thousands of animals a year. Shelters that have a full-service policy never turn an animal away for any reason. This is because most private shelters are founded on a specific philosophy regarding the care and treatment of animals. However, the dilemma is that these shelters are often forced to euthanize animals (kill them painlessly and humanely) after a certain period of time because capacity is not limitless. Other shelters are more selective about what animals they take in, allowing them the ability to refrain from euthanizing unless an animal cannot be saved or is destined to suffer if kept alive. Some take in only cats or dogs; others take in any type of animal, but only those that they deem to be quickly adoptable. If you decide to work in a private shelter, you might want to check the guiding philosophy regarding the animal shelter's policies before you apply.

Because so many animals are brought to animal shelters every year, the shelter has to be well organized on many different levels, which allows for a variety of career opportunities and responsibilities. The following are some of the positions usually found in animal shelters.

Administrators

In a typical private shelter, administrators might include both executive and administrative directors. Many humane societies have a volunteer board of directors to whom the administrative head reports.

The executive director is the overall administrator for the organization and operation of all departments and programs in the private shelter. These departments may include humane education, shelter management, fund-raising, public relations, operation of a veterinary clinic, and field service. As spokesperson for the shelter, the executive director may be called on to be interviewed for local radio and television shows or newspapers, to give testimony at public hearings, or to speak at community gatherings.

The administrative director may work more directly with fundraising programs and membership recruitment and may also be in charge of personnel and selected programs. For either job, a bachelor's degree, or experience in business administration, is extremely helpful. As in any business, the administrator must be adept in communication skills, both written and oral; capable of working well with people; and well organized in order to ensure the smooth operation of the shelter.

As the administrator of a private shelter, you should also have training or experience in animal shelter management. You may become executive director as a result of a promotion from within the shelter, or you may be brought in from the outside if you are an exceptionally qualified candidate, such as a veterinarian with experience in operating an animal clinic or hospital. A commercial kennel manager may also qualify for the executive director position.

Shelter Managers

Many private shelters also have a shelter manager who oversees the daily operation of the kennels, hires and supervises kennel staff, and establishes and maintains procedures for the kennels. A business or liberal arts education could help a person become a shelter manager, but an animal caretaker could also be promoted into the position.

If you are currently an animal caretaker, it would be a good idea to take night courses or attend workshops in animal science, business administration, management, or related topics in order to be considered for promotion to shelter manager since supervisory skills are required for this job.

Shelter managers usually report directly to the executive director and may have at least one assistant manager reporting to them. Together, the shelter manager and assistant manager supervise receiving agents and kennel attendants. Receiving agents are those employees who take the animals in and, if necessary, perform euthanasia. In some animal shelters, the manager or assistant managers also serve as adoption counselors. In this role they screen and interview applicants for part of the day and take care of the animals for the rest of the day.

Assistant shelter managers could be promoted to shelter manager, especially if they had some previous experience in veterinary technology, animal science, kennel management, or animal husbandry. Salaries are relatively low and vary according to location and facility; median hourly earnings were $8.15 in 2004.

Humane Investigators

Some private shelters employ humane investigators (sometimes called agents or cruelty investigators) who investigate reports of animal abuse, negligence, or abandonment. Most states have laws prescribing the training, licensing, and work of these investigators. Some have police powers (can issue citations or warnings to offenders and even assist in the prosecution of offenders) while others do not and must always act in concert with a law enforcement officer when citations are warranted.

Humane investigators generally need a high school education, but specialized programs are not offered at most colleges at the undergraduate level. However, if you are interested in becoming a humane investigator, you might study animal science or veterinary technology, in addition to courses in criminology or law enforcement. Most states require certification, and investigators typically are employed or sponsored by a local private shelter. Some law enforcement officers (police officers or sheriff's deputies) can be certified, giving the enforcement of humane statutes in a community more stature.

In small or rural communities, humane investigators often find only part-time employment. Salaries vary, and promotions are possible for humane investigators, generally to some kind of supervisory investigative position or to assistant shelter manager or shelter manager.

Animal Caretakers

Although caretakers generally are not required to have specialized training, they can attend workshops through various professional organizations. They include the Humane Society of the United States, the American Humane Association, the National Animal Control Association, and state humane associations and animal control associations. Topics include animal handling, kennel sanitation, and methods of humane euthanasia.

A great deal of the caretakers' work involves working with people in a distraught state, so they must have empathy and patience. Caretakers often have to keep records of the animals in their charge, screen applicants for adoption, and vaccinate the animals.

The outlook for animal caretakers is good through 2014, especially in animal shelters, but pay will remain comparatively low. The median hourly salary is $8.39, with some earning as little as $7.16 and others as much as $10.50.

Shelter Veterinarians and Technicians

Private animal shelters also sometimes have veterinary clinics that are headed by a chief veterinarian, to whom other veterinarians and technicians report. The clinic may also use interns from a local college or university to work along with the professionals.

Veterinarians and technicians from a private shelter clinic often operate a low-cost, mobile spay/neuter clinic that travels around the community. One of the major tasks for veterinarians at an animal shelter is to spay and neuter, and they have to be prepared to handle a tremendous volume of this type of work, which a veterinarian in a private practice may not experience.

Volunteer Coordinators

Most private shelters, because they are usually nonprofit organizations, depend on a dedicated group of volunteers on whom they can call for a variety of challenges, chores, and responsibilities. These volunteers may eventually decide to make working with animals a career, as many do. In charge of training and assigning these volunteers is the volunteer coordinator, who is usually a paid staff member but occasionally a volunteer. This position requires organizational as well as communication skills, plus an ability to work well with and supervise others.

Two jobs that volunteers might be involved in are working for a pet therapy program and staffing the phones on a pet-care hotline. The animal behaviorist on staff usually assists in training volunteers for these programs. Pet therapy programs bring volunteers and animals to hospitals and senior citizens' homes so that sick and infirm people get a temporary pet to cuddle. Sometimes emotionally disturbed children are brought to the animal shelter for caring sessions with the animals. On pet-care hotlines, volunteers counsel pet owners over the phone about the pet's behavior and training. Although these volunteers work closely with other professional staff people, they are assigned and scheduled by the volunteer coordinator.

Office Support Staff

No smoothly operating organization can function without efficient support staff. Administrative assistants and file and records clerks are needed at most animal shelters. Those at the front desk are sometimes called customer service agents because they are the first contact the public has with the agency. They may also serve as file clerks. In some animal shelters, they issue identification tags to the animals, record all pertinent data about an animal onto cards, and provide information about adoption procedures to the public.

Although not all clerical positions in the animal shelter require direct contact with animals, front desk personnel should be able to work well with people, who are sometimes upset over the loss of an animal, and with the animals that they may be checking in for adoption. In these cases, empathy and compassion can prove important qualities to have.

Clerical workers should be able to use computers and be familiar with business software, such as word processing, scheduling, accounting, and database programs. They must be able to operate other business machines, such as photocopiers, calculators, mail-sorting machines, and postage meters.

The outlook for jobs for clerical workers in humane societies is good, especially if you have a high school diploma and a basic knowledge of grammar, spelling, punctuation, and mathematics. Reliability, cooperation, punctuality, and organizational skills are also looked upon favorably by potential employers.

Humane Educators

Many humane societies believe so strongly in educating the public, especially children, about the humane treatment of animals that the humane educator has become a specialized title in humane animal work. The humane education department of a private shelter upholds and implements the philosophy of the individual agency, which may differ between agencies. Mainly, though, humane educators stress kindness and compassion to all living beings, animal care, pet overpopulation, and safety around animals, including bite prevention.

Reaching Out to the Public. Most humane societies send their educators out into the grade schools of their communities to teach children about values, attitudes, pet care, and animal awareness. Working with students in all grades of one school over a period of three to five days, the educator covers many topics, such as animal needs, dangers to animals, overpopulation problems and solutions, and the general responsibilities of pet owners. In the upper grades, the students are told about the work of a private shelter and careers with animals. Usually tours of the animal shelter can also be arranged. More than twenty states consider humane education so important that they have enacted laws for compulsory classroom humane education.

In addition to making these presentations, humane educators also provide teachers and students with informational handouts and packets. Some animal shelters, depending on their sizes and budgets, produce periodic newsletters, videos, and tapes for school use. Other humane educators use materials produced by either the national animal welfare organizations—American Humane Association (AHA), American Society for the Prevention of Cruelty to Animals (ASPCA), the Humane Society of the United States (HSUS)—or national organizations that focus specifically on humane education, such as the National Association for Humane and Environmental Education (NAHEE).

The Humane Education Department. Larger humane societies located in big cities generally have humane education departments, to which the humane educator belongs. The department is headed by a director who coordinates all humane education programs, including those involving schools, libraries, museums, and other animal shelters. The director also deals with personnel problems and usually reports directly to the executive director or administrative director.

Educating the Educator. If you are considering a career as a humane educator, you should have a college degree in education or a related field. A minor in animal science is helpful, as well as courses in journalism, outdoor recreation, public relations, or environmental education. To become director of a humane education department, you may need a master's degree in education. At this level, courses in management, writing, and public speaking are desirable. Contact NAHEE, listed at the end of this chapter, for more information on regional workshops in this field. As a humane educator, your salary varies with the size of the facility and community. Generally, larger animal shelters within larger cities offer the highest salaries, as well as more opportunities for jobs and promotions.

A Humane Education Director

John Caruso, director of humane education for a large private shelter, majored in English and philosophy in college, not animal husbandry or biology. He says he was not one of those children who brought home stray cats and dogs. But he feels strongly that a thorough liberal arts background is valuable for anyone in humane education because it can help people analyze situations and solve problems—abilities that are needed in a management position.

John also had some background in public speaking and theater, so when he applied for a job in customer service at the animal shelter, they thought he was better suited to education. He served as an educator under three separate managers, each of whom had a distinctive approach to the job. When the manager position became available, he applied and, because of his on-the-job training, became manager and finally director.

Because he is a manager, John does not have direct contact with animals and thus has no need for scientific training. Humane educators often begin at private shelters as volunteers or kennel attendants because many animal shelters have a policy of promoting from within. This in-house promotion policy is a strong drawing point for volunteers and entry-level employees and helps compensate for generally low pay. John believes that, in addition, most animal shelters offer good benefits packages and sometimes tuition-reimbursement programs for those who wish to continue their education.

Humane educators at the animal shelter give presentations to more than forty thousand students annually. In addition, they generate all kinds of written material and often handle more than two hundred calls on pet behavior per month. John and his staff feel that the work they do is important and helps people and animals live more harmoniously together.

Working for Animal Control Agencies

The animal shelters within animal control agencies, typically run by the city or county government, are structured roughly the same as private shelters. They employ veterinarians, technicians, animal care attendants, administrators, and clerical workers, but, in addition, the agency employs animal control officers who work out in the field. However, the primary difference between a private shelter and an animal control agency is in its mandate. Private shelters are established to prevent or lessen suffering and abuse of animals. The primary objective of the animal control agency, on the other hand, is to protect public health and safety by making sure that animals do not impinge on the lives of the residents of the community.

The legal responsibilities of animal control agencies include patrolling for stray animals; impounding them according to local laws; and investigating residents' complaints about animal-related noises and odors, injuries inflicted by animals, and property damage caused by pets or strays.

Director of Animal Control

The animal control agency is headed by the director of animal control, who functions as the chief administrator. The director is responsible for all agency programs and personnel.

Job qualifications and education for this position are generally the same as for the executive director of a private shelter. Because the public agency is funded by the government, however, there is no real need for fund-raising talents. Animal control directors, as government employees, must know and uphold the animal control laws of their individual communities.

Animal Control Officers

Animal control officers were sometimes formerly called dog catchers. The animal control officer may be called on to rescue trapped animals, conduct obedience and pet-care classes, enforce licensing laws, and investigate possible animal abuse cases. In some states, animal control officers are authorized to inspect pet shops, boarding facilities, horse stables, and other businesses to see that the owners are complying with animal welfare regulations (although in many states much of the responsibility for overseeing animal businesses falls to field officers who work for the state department of agriculture).

If the community has laws about rabies or other inoculations, the animal control officer must enforce them. These officers should also know the rudiments of first aid, especially when dealing with trapped, abused, or injured animals. Animal control officers may have to work with other government departments, such as the police or health departments; environmental, wildlife, or conservation agencies; and with private shelters.

Their focus is on public health and safety and protection of animals and their owners through education, intervention, and law enforcement. They work in the field, in the animal shelter, and in the community. Animal control shelters are run like private shelters and usually have the same staffing requirements.

When it becomes necessary for the animal control officer to bring in stray animals for impoundment, the strays are turned over to the shelter manager, who keeps records of all animals in the kennels. Kennel attendants then see to the daily care, feeding, and cleaning of the animals, just as in a private shelter. This is usually where euthanasia takes place, if that becomes necessary. Some animal control shelters run adoption programs, spay/neuter clinics, and public education programs much as humane societies do. When funding and support are available for these programs, they clearly benefit public health and safety. Children who know how to safely approach strange dogs are less likely to be bitten; families that understand the importance of spaying and neutering are less likely to become nuisance households in their neighborhoods.

Education Requirements

Entry-level animal control officers are usually required to have a high school diploma or GED. Any additional undergraduate courses you take to prepare for this job should include criminology and some animal science or veterinary technology training. You receive further training when you are hired, usually from an experienced agent. A euthanasia technician certificate is required for most jobs. In addition, math, science, English, zoology, and computer classes are needed. Some study of law enforcement and safety is also helpful. This kind of work demands not only knowledge of local animal ordinances but also an ability to make good judgments and to cope with the stress imposed by the fieldwork.

Earnings and Outlook

As with most career paths, management positions in animal control command the highest annual salaries—from $50,000 to $85,000 in large cities; $30,000 to $45,000 in mid-sized cities; and about $24,000 in smaller communities. Entry-level positions may start at minimum wage and increase with additional or specialized training. Again, salaries and opportunities at all levels are usually better in larger cities.

Working in Wildlife Refuges and Rehabilitation Centers

Wildlife is defined as all animals that are not domesticated. Fish may be included in this definition. The entire field of wildlife management in this country is less than one hundred years old. It is generally defined as the human maintenance and manipulation of natural resources to benefit the total environment. In that broad context, the saving of individual animals and the protection and preservation of entire species is vital. Wildlife and its preservation are important to the ecological balance of the planet. Efforts at maintaining this balance are becoming increasingly important in these times of greater and greater environmental pollution and increased habitat destruction.

Wildlife Refuges

Many positions in wildlife management are to be found in wildlife refuges. These refuges may be public or private, with most being run by either state, federal, or provincial (Canadian) governmental agencies. Wildlife refuges provide shelter for endangered species, protect those species that are threatened, and study habitat and diseases of wildlife.

Careers in wildlife management at refuges often require arduous study and training, long hours, determination, and a deep commitment to the protection and preservation of individual animals and whole species.

Refuges must have an organizational structure if they are to run smoothly. Therefore, they need administrators and clerical workers, wildlife and research biologists, and often fishery biologists. Veterinarians and volunteer coordinators may round out the staffing.

Refuge Managers. The U.S. Fish and Wildlife Service of the Department of the Interior runs hundreds of wildlife refuges across the country. Refuge managers' responsibilities are primarily to protect indigenous and migratory fish and wildlife and to control and regulate hunting and fishing at the refuges. The manager is a highly skilled professional who has probably come up through the ranks and who has a great deal of technical knowledge. However, as an administrator, the manager also must have a good business sense, work well with people, and know how to stretch a budget dollar.

Managers should have a college degree, preferably in a physical or biological science. Specifically, they should have completed nine hours of zoology and six hours in wildlife courses. Managers should also have a mastery of English, including speaking, reading, and writing. Psychology, geography, public relations, and economics courses are also very helpful.

If you are still in high school and are thinking of wildlife management as a career, you should study math, English, chemistry, and biology. Any experience working on committees, conducting meetings, or writing for newspapers or yearbooks will also help.

Because wildlife work is highly competitive, you are encouraged to get a master's degree or a doctorate in wildlife-related fields to increase your chances of employment. Many colleges and universities in North America now offer courses leading to a degree in wildlife management.

Wildlife Biologists. Wildlife biologists study wildlife distribution, habitat, ecology, mortality, and economic value. In addition, they conduct wildlife programs, apply results of research to wildlife management, work with the restoration or creation of wildlife habitats, and help to control diseases in wildlife.

Wildlife biologists working as research scientists have to be knowledgeable about wildlife population dynamics, land use, and environmental pollution. Their primary training must be in the scientific method of collecting, analyzing, and objectively reporting data to their supervisors and other refuges for future practical applications.

Fishery biologists work with aquatic organisms in fish hatcheries where rearing and stocking operations are performed. Habitat, history, and classification of these organisms are also part of the study of fishery biologists.

Wildlife biologists should have a college degree with at least thirty semester hours in biology. These would include nine hours in wildlife-related subjects, twelve hours in zoology, and nine hours in botany. For more information on wildlife management, see Chapter 8.

Rehabilitation Centers

Animal rehabilitation centers, operated by private or public agencies, are devoted to the treatment of sick or injured wildlife. Many specialize in one species or one type of animal within a species. Rehabilitation centers are necessary because all forms of wildlife are subject to natural disasters as well as human-caused hazards. Wild animals suffer during tornadoes, blizzards, earthquakes, and droughts. They are sickened by oil spills and water and air pollution. They are injured or wounded by traps, gunshots, collisions, live wires, and natural predators. And they are subject to disease, just as humans are.

Rehabilitation centers usually are headed by a professional manager and employ wildlife or fishery biologists and volunteer coordinators. Educational requirements are similar to those for positions in the refuge, but for those biologists who work directly with injured animals, special emphasis may be placed on training or course work in clinical pathology, basic shock cycles, anatomy and physiology, drug dosage, physical therapy, and emergency care. Clinical pathology courses include some laboratory procedures in blood work, parasitology, and urinalysis in wild animals. You will be taught how to draw blood, test white cell counts, and test for heartworm.

To work in a rehabilitation center, you will need to know how to treat wounds, heal fractures, and determine antibiotic treatments. If you work with birds, you must be able to clean and care for birds caught and injured in oil spills. Some tasks in a rehabilitation center are more complex, such as setting up a physical therapy program for a particular kind of animal. Some wildlife biologists working at rehabilitation centers exclusively perform research into various ways of reducing the incidence and spread of fatal diseases in wildlife.

Volunteer coordinators can learn the specific skills they need to perform their jobs at workshops and seminars. Such courses might focus on recruiting, training, motivating, and delegating, as well as burnout management.

The International Wildlife Rehabilitation Council is the professional organization to contact for further information in this field. Members include administrators, educators, researchers, veterinarians, and humane workers. Although it is not a licensing agency, it does offer certified course work in various aspects of animal rehabilitation.

Is Shelter or Refuge Work for You?

Now you should have a better idea of the opportunities that are available in animal shelters, animal control agencies, wildlife refuges, and rehabilitation centers. If you are still interested in exploring these possibilities, you need to make a few basic decisions. They will revolve around whether you want to work for a public or private agency; how much time you want to devote to education and training; which kind of animal, domesticated or wild, you wish to care for every day; whether you want to be an administrator or a fieldworker; and what your philosophy is about the care and treatment of animals.

Whatever your choice, keep in mind that direct work with any animal in need of help can be stressful and even traumatic. Your physical and emotional strength, compassion, and technical skills will be necessary to see you through the long hours of difficult work. But you should also be aware that the rewards are equal to or outweigh the difficulties. Your work is essential to the well-being of all creatures—including humans.

For More Information

Publications

Animal Sheltering magazine. The Humane Society of the United States.

Handy, Geoffry L. *Animal Control Management: A Guide for Local Governments*. International City/County Management Association, 2001.

Hess, Elizabeth. *Lost and Found: Dogs, Cats, and Everyday Heroes at a Country Animal Shelter*. Harvest Books, 2006.

The Humane Society of the United States: John Hadidian, Guy R. Hodge, John W. Grandy, editors. *Wild Neighbors: The Humane Approach to Living with Wildlife*. Fulcrum Publishing, 1997.

National Audubon Society. *Book of Wild Animals*. Wings Books, 1996.

Unti, Bernard Oreste. *Protecting All Animals: A Fifty-Year History of the Humane Society of the United States*. Humane Society Press, 2004.

Williams, Terrie M., and Randall Davis, editors. *Emergency Care and Rehabilitation of Oiled Sea Otters: A Guide for Oil Spills Involving Fur-Bearing Marine Mammals*. University of Alaska Press, 1995.

Associations

American Humane Association (AHA)
63 Inverness Drive East
Englewood, CO 80112
www.americanhumane.org

American Society for the Prevention of Cruelty to Animals
  (ASPCA)
424 East Ninety-Second Street
New York, NY 10128
www.aspca.org

Center for Animals and Public Policy
Tufts School of Veterinary Medicine
200 Westboro Road
North Grafton, MA 01536
www.tufts.edu/vet/cfa

The Humane Society of Canada
The Atrium on Bay
40 Dundas Street West, Suite 227B
PO Box 16
Toronto, ON M5G 2CZ
Canada
www.humanesociety.com

The Humane Society of the United States (HSUS)
2100 L Street NW
Washington, DC 20037
www.hsus.org

International Wildlife Rehabilitation Council
PO Box 8187
San Jose, CA 95155
www.iwrc-online.org

National Animal Control Association
PO Box 480851
Kansas City, MO 64148
www.nacanet.org

National Association for Humane and Environmental
  Education (NAHEE)
67 Norwich Essex Turnpike
East Haddam, CT 06423
www.nahee.org

National Humane Education Society
PO Box 340
Charles Town, WV 25414
www.nhes.org

National Wildlife Rehabilitator's Association
2625 Clearwater Road, Suite 110
St. Cloud, MN 56301
www.nwrawildlife.org

CHAPTER FOUR

But Can Cats Be Trained?

Maybe your particular strengths and aptitudes lie in teaching an animal to behave, to perform certain tricks, to guard the house, or to provide guidance for people with disabilities. Many people develop the rudiments of obedience training skills with their first pet. You may have been able to make your dog sit, stay, or keep off the couch.

On the other hand, you may have lived in a rural area, becoming familiar with horses and how to handle them. You may have been fascinated by trained animals in the movies or dolphins at the zoo. You may have even performed the miraculous—trained a cat to jump through a hoop!

If any of these descriptions fit you, there are opportunities in the field of animal training. Again, you must decide which animals you prefer to deal with and which kind of training you would be best at. Then you can set your course accordingly. No matter which type of training and animal you choose, you must genuinely like animals and have the ability to communicate with them and their owners. That often requires patience, physical endurance, and a basic knowledge of psychology.

Your love of the work will often have to compensate for low pay, and your natural talents and abilities must, of course, be honed into actual technical skills, which can be acquired in several ways. For some, college courses are the key to successful employment in animal training. Others learn training skills in the military or law enforcement agencies. Still others start out as volunteers or apprentices to a professional trainer or work at shows to gain experience. Others have combined these methods and natural talents to create a career. If you plan to work with exotic animals or those with specific behavioral problems, or if you plan to work in zoos, you may be required to have a college degree in animal science, zoology, or animal behavior. If you choose to train marine animals, you must be a strong swimmer and may need a degree in marine biology, zoology, or psychology.

Dog Trainers

Probably the greatest number of animal trainers in the field today are dog trainers. Because of the popularity of dogs as pets, trainers are called upon to teach them how to behave and follow owners' instructions. Training methods may vary, but generally the pet learns not to chew up the furniture or articles of clothing, not to sleep on the furniture, and not to run into the street. They also learn how to walk on a leash and to sit, stay, and lie down on command. Some pets may have deeper problems that may contribute to inappropriate behavior, such as aggression.

Some trainers deal exclusively with animals that are boarded at the training facility during the training period. Others conduct classes with owners and pets together. Some trainers work for larger training centers; others are self-employed. Some work as trainers full-time; others, only part-time. Those who are full-time, self-employed trainers may supply other services, such as boarding and selling food and training supplies. They may also provide counseling to people who are about to purchase a pet dog and give advice on nutrition for the pet.

Gaining Experience as a Dog Trainer

It is possible to become a dog trainer by combining your basic aptitude with on-the-job training. If you feel that animal training is the career you want to pursue, you could begin as a part-time volunteer at a training facility. The facility could be a larger training academy or a smaller private business.

Different kinds of facilities may have different qualifications for employment. They may, for instance, require that you have previous experience with animals or animal-related education, or they may prefer to train you totally in their own methods. As an apprentice, you may be required to work for up to five years under the supervision of an experienced trainer. You should exercise extreme caution in selecting trainers to apprentice with. You should investigate their training methods and inquire about any certification they may have or professional organizations they belong to. Your professional reputation as a trainer may well hinge upon your choice of instructor.

Education for Dog Trainers

More and more people who choose animal training are opting for some kind of college education related to the job. College course work might include psychology, animal behavior, animal science, or veterinary technology as a basis. This formal education will enhance your on-the-job training and put you in a better position for employment.

Attending dog training academies is yet another route to employment as a trainer. These courses are usually fairly short, however, and sometimes insubstantial, with the trainee acting largely as a kennel attendant. There is usually just some very basic instruction in actual animal training. You should be wary of these academies because they are typically quite expensive and may not be accredited.

Training Guide Dogs

As a dog trainer, your instruction is not limited to pet behavior problems. You may, for example, want to specialize in training guide dogs to help blind people lead more independent lives.

There are only a few places in the country that train guide dogs, so the competition for job openings can be fierce. In order to qualify for employment as a guide dog trainer, you must be physically strong and have previous work experience with animals. It is preferable to have an educational background in veterinary technology, animal science, or to have work experience in a boarding or breeding kennel, animal hospital, or farm.

Most guide dog trainers agree that golden retrievers and Labrador retrievers, or a cross between them, are the best breeds for this work. As puppies, they are usually trained in basic obedience and real-world experience by puppy walkers. After several months, they are brought to guide dog school for about sixteen months, where the dogs are tested for suitability. If a dog passes the test, it goes on to harness training for about three months. Then blind students are brought in to work with the trainers and the dog. Only after an additional three months are owner and dog ready to go it alone.

Most people are familiar with guide dogs for the blind, which are now quite common. But deaf people need help, too—in getting around, waking up on time, and knowing when the telephone or doorbell rings. Even such basic security devices as smoke detectors, sirens, and fire alarms are geared to people who can hear. Life can be dangerous for people who cannot hear these sounds and whose freedom of movement is restricted.

Enter the dog who acts as its owner's ears. These dogs must be able to differentiate sounds and signal the owner appropriately, according to whether the sound is an alarm clock or a smoke detector. They have to be alert and energetic, healthy and vigorous. Trainers of such dogs need both people and animal skills in order to match owners to dogs and consider the individual personalities and needs of both.

Often these dogs have been rescued from the pound. They usually go through training for more than a year with a hearing-impaired handler before handler and dog are able to work as a team. Professional organizations can help you find the training program that's right for you and inform you of the required qualifications.

Training Working Dogs

The U.S. Customs Service, the military, law enforcement, and other government agencies employ animal trainers and handlers to train animals, mainly dogs, for such tasks as detecting specific scents at border crossings or airport terminals, finding injured people trapped in wreckage caused by earthquakes or other disasters, and even attacking enemies. These agencies usually train their own personnel and thus often require no specialized education or training experience for employment. The dogs that are trained as guard dogs, either for law enforcement agencies or private owners, must have obedience training first. The best dogs for this type of training should be aggressive but obedient. Therefore, you would probably be working with such breeds as German shepherds, Doberman pinschers, or rottweilers.

These dogs usually begin training with the handler at the kennel at the age of three to four months. Then they are brought to the actual work site to continue their training. Dogs who guard homes should be good barkers because that is what usually deters burglars; however, they must be gentle and loving pets, too. But guard-dog trainers can train the dogs to bite and attack on command if their work calls for that type of action.

Handling Show Dogs

Dog handlers are used to show animals at dog shows. They usually work with individual dogs. Aspiring show dog handlers must have several years of experience working with owners and exhibitors of purebreds in order to qualify for apprenticeship with an experienced handler. As professional show handlers, they often show dogs for those who do not know how or are too busy to show their own animals.

A Professional Dog Trainer

Jim Morgan, a professional dog trainer in a large Midwestern city, opened his own training facility after running his business from the back of a Chevette. He used to load up his little car with dogs of all sizes and bring them to the park to train. During this period, he was trying to build a full-time business, based largely on a lot of natural talent and a real desire to turn that talent into a livelihood. He was not sure that anyone could really earn a living training dogs because he found it so easy that he had a hard time believing that anyone couldn't do it.

Jim thinks the demand for professional obedience training for pets came about when women started to work outside the home. Often in the past, Mom stayed at home and was able to housebreak the family dog and teach it to sit, fetch, heel, and walk on a leash.

Now Jim and his wife and children live upstairs, and the dogs they train and board live downstairs in what Jim considers to be the perfect arrangement—the dogs are never alone, and he doesn't have to worry about them if they should get sick or need attention. He specializes in obedience training, but because of his customers' fears of break-ins and street crime, about 10 percent of his business is devoted to protection training.

Jim has evolved his own unique training methods and style. And because he is self-employed, he can set his own fees. Jim thinks that people in high school or college should consider taking biology, animal science, or any preveterinary courses to prepare for a career as a trainer. And he believes that anyone who wants to work with dogs has to go to dog shows, attend obedience training classes, work in kennels, read dog-related publications, and talk to everyone he or she can in the field. He would urge anyone who is considering this career to volunteer or work part-time caring for dogs, observing other trainers, and asking questions.

Jim warns anyone who wants to learn how to train dogs to be very careful about false claims and deceptive practices. Dog-related publications carry advertisements for dog training academies and schools, but Jim thinks that if you decide to attend these courses, you should find out the names of recent graduates and whether they are presently working as trainers. In other words, you should find out if those who have completed the course are competent and employable. Professional standards for accreditation and certification of licensed trainers is becoming the norm. People considering dog training as a career should keep up with this trend toward professionalism so that they can fulfill the requirements set forth in those standards.

The mission of the National Association of Dog Obedience Instructors, for example, is to provide continuing education while endorsing dog obedience trainers of the highest caliber and to continue to promote humane, effective training methods and competent instructors. The Association of Pet Dog Trainers is also committed to the continuing education of trainers. Both organizations have members throughout the world.

If you are thinking about training dogs for a living, you also need to be aware that you will be dealing with human owners. That part of the job is the most difficult for Jim and is why he insists that the dog stay with him for a two-week training period —without the owner. During that time, the owner is only allowed to view the dog at a distance for example, from the car while the dog is being trained in the park. Jim believes in training every dog individually and in establishing rapport with the animal before the actual commands are taught. With some dogs, Jim achieves almost instant rapport; other dogs catch on only at the last minute.

Jim prefers to train dogs when they are young while they still have nothing that needs to be unlearned. After the dog is trained, he offers weekly owners' classes to reinforce training or to teach the dogs new commands. Jim has never had to advertise his services—satisfied customers let others know of his skill and pass it on by word of mouth to family, friends, and neighbors. He has trained thousands of dogs and suggests that to make a living in dog training, you must love dogs, love working with them, and be prepared to work long and hard. But in spite of the hard work, so far Jim wouldn't dream of having it any other way.

Horse Trainers

Those who choose to train horses take many of the same entry paths as dog trainers: apprenticeship under a professional trainer, educational background in animal science or technology, or experience as a volunteer or hobbyist. Once you have entered one of these paths, you need to determine where and what you want to train.

If you decide to come up through the ranks, you will be able to learn in farms, stables, or racetracks. On the other hand, a college education will train you in many of the skills you need and give you some practical experience. It may also improve your existing skills.

You will have to decide on the kind of horse you feel most comfortable with—saddle horse, quarter horse, or Lipizzan, among others. You will then want to decide whether you want to train horses for steeplechase, dressage, racing, or show jumping. With any of these choices, you also should be able to work well with people—the riders, who are also being trained, and the owners of the horses. All of these options require determination, endurance, patience, physical strength, and, of course, a love of horses.

Horse training is different from dog training because the emphasis is not on behavior or protection, but rather on performing specific tasks for competition and prizes. Racehorses, for example, long part of our cultural scene, require specialized training because the owner's prestige (and often livelihood) is at stake. Amateur equestrians depend on the horse's training for international competitions that may lead to professional standing. And all of these events and competitions depend on the competency of the trainer who will prepare the horse and rider for the specific purpose they are capable of and designate as their goal.

Cat Trainers

For most of us, dog and horse training seem familiar. We know that dogs and horses love to be trained to perform, protect, or compete. But what about cats? "Never!" you say. But if you really want to train your cat to play a toy piano, roll over and play dead, sit up and beg, or jump through a hoop, you might take some advice from George Ney.

A Cat Trainer's Story

George Ney was hit hard by economic downturns. When the housing industry foundered, his business as a tile and carpeting salesperson also began to fall apart.

Being a creative person, however, George used some of that unused carpeting and started to build cat houses, including condos, duplexes, and ranch styles, as well as couches, chairs, lamps, and tables. In order to sell them, he brought them to cat shows, where he became moderately successful and fairly well known for his imaginative designs.

Eventually, and instinctively, George had begun to try some basic tricks with one of his cats. Surprisingly, the cat learned to roll over, to beg, and to shake hands. When he told people about this performing cat, they all laughed in disbelief—until they saw it for themselves.

George began putting on volunteer demonstrations at local establishments and then bringing the act to cat shows, where he and the cat performed. He also sold some of his cat furniture. Eventually he taught the cat more and more tricks, such as sitting in a high chair, rolling a barrel, and "answering" a toy telephone. He added more cats and traveled most weekends with his feline troupe, logging about forty thousand miles a year. They have appeared in malls, convention halls, schools, nursing homes, on television, and in commercials—proving that training cats is not impossible.

Advice on How to Train Your Cat. George's training methods and style are based on love and fun. They include gentleness, pacing, and patience. George learned that cats' attention spans are not long. Training sessions don't last more than ten minutes in an hour, but they are held as many times during the day as possible, between catnaps. Working with natural feline abilities, such as jumping and rolling, as well as a love of petting, George devised ways to make cats respond to certain cues. He also learned to reduce the larger trick down into its simpler component parts.

Some of the problems with training cats originate in humans' misunderstanding of cats. They are really not as aloof and independent as some think, but they certainly lack the inclination toward training that dogs and horses have. George believes that you should start with a neutered cat who already knows how to use a litter pan. He suggests you start training a cat with simple tasks, such as using a scratching post or staying off the furniture. Catnip and a water spray are usually enough to teach most cats what you require as acceptable behavior.

To learn tricks, your cat should be at least eight weeks old and enjoy being touched and petted. You need to pay attention and let the cat give you cues as to its fatigue, boredom, or lack of interest in any particular trick. Repetition, praise, and a training table to practice on are essential components in the training of cats.

If you are planning to make a living with your trained cats, you also have to be sure that your cats can travel well and can adapt to the changes of life on the road. Cats are usually very territorial and can be very upset by changes in their environment, including noises. You might consider training more animals than you actually bring with you to any given show, so that they can have a resting period between trips.

Because there is no market for watch cats or any need for cats to protect home or property, training cats to perform should be considered a method of bonding between owner and cat and a source of pleasure for both. George Ney decided to make a career of it. He literally created this career out of economic necessity and love and thus had no previous formal training or education, either in making cat furniture or training cats. But as a businessperson, he was concerned with publicity and promotion, booking and scheduling, travel and veterinarian expenses. Being affiliated with professional associations such as the American Cat Fanciers Association, Canadian Cat Association, International Cat Association, and Cat Fanciers' Association is very helpful in such a career. Cat periodicals tell trainers when and where national shows are taking place, and local papers and bulletins inform them of local events and organizations that may be sources of future business.

As with many careers dealing with animals, there are often no established educational and training criteria and standards. Sometimes you just have to combine natural talent, economic necessity, hard work, and love of animals to create a career path that provides you with economic security, a real sense of satisfaction, pleasure, and fun.

More Options for Animal Trainers

You may decide to apply your training talents exclusively to the performing arts, such as movies, television commercials and shows, special events and performances, circuses, and carnivals. The animals you train might include dogs, cats, horses, elephants, lions, and tigers. Often zoological parks or aquariums have performing animals as part of their exhibits, and trained animals may also appear at trade fairs and shows, parties, and community events.

You may work as an independent contractor who hires out to movie or television producers, zookeepers, aquarium curators, or show organizers to teach specialized tricks to specific animals. Or a particular animal may be used as the regular representative of a particular product or service in a continuing series of television commercials.

As an independent contractor, you may set your own per diem or per performance fee. Fees vary according to the venue, such as performing at a children's party or for a commercial or movie. If one of your animals has a major role in a movie or is the star of a commercial series, your fee might be quite high. If you are employed by a particular institution on a regular basis, you may receive an annual salary with normal benefits.

Trainers may also decide to write books or articles or even put together audio- or videotapes on successful training techniques and unusual experiences. They also may combine their training skills with other services, such as counseling, nutritional advice, kennel operation, or pet product sales.

Some trainers choose to use their experiences and skills as a stepping-stone to other positions within their fields or to open up their own franchise operations or combination shops. As you gain experience and a solid reputation, you may begin to train apprentices. And as professional organizations start up, you may become involved in their work.

These choices are up to you, according to your inclinations and capabilities. Decide which animal you are most comfortable with—dogs, cats, horses, marine mammals, or exotic animals. Do you want to train them for specific skills? Do you want to work for another person or be an independent contractor? Are you willing to be on call for the animals every day, all day? Would you like a combination business, such as trainer and kennel operator? Do you want to train guide dogs or police dogs? There's just one thing you should be sure of before you decide to become either a trainer or handler: you must *love* to work with animals!

Employment Outlook

The demand for qualified animal trainers is good within the public and private sectors. The Bureau of Labor Statistics projects growth until 2012 as between 10 percent and 20 percent, with an additional nine thousand employees needed in that time frame. The median annual wage is $24,400.

As an employee of a federal or local government agency, your salary is set according to your job category, and you can count on a fair amount of job security. Self-employed trainers can set their own fees and hours, which often are long and irregular.

For More Information

Publications

Blake, Henry. *Horse Sense: How to Develop Your Horse's Intelligence.* Trafalgar Square Publishing, 1994.

Clark, Gail I., and William N. Boyer. *The Mentally Sound Dog: How to Shape, Train & Change Canine Behavior.* Alpine Publications, 1995.

Davis, Kathy Diamond. *Therapy Dogs: Training Your Dog to Help Others.* Dogwise Publishing, 2002.

Esordi, Renee Lamm. *You Have a Visitor: Observations on Pet Visitation and Therapy.* Blue Lamm Publishing, 2000.

Fogle, Bruce. *ASPCA Dog Training.* D K Publishing, 1999.

Frost, April, and Rondi Lightmark. *Beyond Obedience: Training with Awareness for You & Your Dog.* Three Rivers Press, 1999.

Helgren, J. Anne. *Communicating with Your Cat.* Barron's Educational Series, 1999.

Hoffman, Martha. *Lend Me an Ear: The Temperament, Selection and Training of the Hearing Dog.* Doral Publishing, 1999.

Mackay, Nicci. *Spoken in Whispers: The Autobiography of a Horse Whisperer.* Fireside, 1997.

Miller, Pat. *The Power of Positive Dog Training*. Howell Book
House, 2001.

Mills, Daniel S., and Kathryn Nankervis. *Equine Behavior:
Principles & Practice*. Blackwell Publishing, 1998.

Murphy, Jana. *The Secret Lives of Dogs: The Real Reasons Behind
52 Mysterious Canine Behaviors*. Rodale Press, 2000.

Palika, Liz. *Love on a Leash: Giving Joy to Others Through Pet
Therapy*. Alpine Publications, 1998.

Rendell, Sharon. *Living with Big Cats: The Story of Jungle Larry,
Safari Jane, and David Tetzlaff*. International Zoological
Society, 1994.

Associations

American Cat Fanciers Association
PO Box 1949
Nixan, MO 65714
www.acfacats.com

Animal Behavior Society
2611 East Tenth Street
Bloomington, IN 47408
www.animalbehavior.org

Association of Pet Dog Trainers
150 Executive Center Drive, Box 35
Greenville, SC 29615
www.apdt.com

Association of Zoos and Aquariums
8403 Colesville Road, Suite 710
Silver Spring, MD 20910
www.aza.org

Canadian Cat Association
289 Rutherford Road, Suite 18
Brampton, ON L6W 3R9
Canada
www.cca-afc.com

Canine Vision
PO Box 907
Oakville, ON L6J 5E8
Canada
www.dogguides.com

Cat Fanciers' Association
PO Box 1005
Manasquan, NJ 08736
www.cfainc.org

Coalition to Protect Animals in Entertainment
1355 Basel Place
Riverside, CA 92506

Dogs for the Deaf
10175 Wheeler Road
Central Point, OR 97502
www.dogsforthedeaf.org

Guide Dog Foundation for the Blind
371 East Jericho Turnpike
Smithtown, NY 11787
www.guidedog.org

Guide Dogs for the Blind
PO Box 151200
San Rafael, CA 94915
www.guidedogs.com

The International Association of Avian Trainers & Educators
350 St. Andrews Fairway
Memphis, TN 38111
www.iaate.org

International Cat Association
PO Box 2684
Harlingen, TX 78551
www.tica.org

International Marine Animal Trainers Association (IMATA)
1200 South Lake Shore Drive
Chicago, IL 60605
www.imata.org

National Association of Dog Obedience Instructors
PMB #369
729 Grapevine Highway
Hurst, TX 76054
www.nadoi.org

National Police Canine Association
PO Box 264
Robert, LA 70455
www.npca.net

North American Police Work Dog Association
4222 Manchester Avenue
Perry, OH 44081
www.napwda.com

Training Programs

Canine Enforcement Training Center
U.S. Customs and Border Protection
1300 Pennsylvania Avenue NW
Washington, DC 20229
www.customs.ustreas.gov/xp/cgov/border_security/canines

Certification Council for Professional Dog Trainers
Professional Testing Corporation
1350 Broadway, Seventeenth Floor
New York, NY 10018
www.ccpdt.org

Exotic Animal Training and Management Program
Moorpark College
7075 Campus Road
Moorpark, CA 93021
www.moorparkcollege.edu/zoo

Guiding Eyes for the Blind
Training School and Headquarters
611 Granite Springs Road
Yorktown Heights, NY 10598
www.guiding-eyes.org

Hollywood Animals
Husbandry and Exotic Animal Training School
4103 Holly Knoll Drive
Los Angeles, CA 90027
www.animalschool.net

Work Dogs International
43455 Hilltop Drive
Banning, CA 92220
www.policedogtrainers.com

Websites

A Career Guide to Marine Mammal Care
www.dolphintrainer.com

Aquafacts: Career as a Marine Mammal Trainer
www.vanaqua.org/education/aquafacts/
   marinemammaltrainer.html

Assistance Dogs International
www.adionline.org

CHAPTER FIVE

Business Opportunities for Animal Lovers

Other people besides veterinarians and shelter workers take care of animals or see to the needs of pet owners. These include the businesspeople who provide supplies and services that maintain animals' health and well-being, take care of pets while owners are away, and even dispose of the pets' remains when they die. At all times between birth and death, animals have needs that must be met, and there is usually a career path associated with these needs.

We will discuss the basic needs of animals and how they can be served and then branch out into more unusual possibilities, including the creation of new careers based on changing needs and technological advances. Then you can decide which possibility fits your own needs, education, inclinations, and talents.

Because business owners are largely entrepreneurial, they can generally determine how much they will charge for their services or supplies depending on whether they are in a large city or small town, whether they cater to a more upscale clientele, how many services they offer, and how much they have to clear in profit after they have earned enough to cover expenses. A survey of local businesses may guide you about prices that are generally charged for similar services, and you can then determine what you will charge.

Neighborhood Pet Supply Stores

The pet supply store is where we find everything related to pets for sale—from cat litter and litter pans to toys, ID tags, and scratching posts; from catnip to cages, collars, and carriers; from food and flea powder to training supplies and shampoo. We also find items that are not for sale—such as advice, nutritional charts, pictures of other pets that have been brought in by customers, notices of lost and found animals, and referrals to professionals in the field, such as veterinarians, breeders, trainers, transporters, sitters, and kennel operators. Over the phone you can receive prices, sometimes friendly counsel, and general, all-around caring conversation to comfort you in your concern for your pet's needs.

Pet Supply Store Owners

In these days of megapet supply stores, it's refreshing to know that a few small, independent neighborhood stores still exist. These are the stores that were started by people who genuinely cared for animals and their needs, and it is comforting to know that they still thrive because of their personal knowledge of the pets and pet owners in the neighborhood.

Such a story belongs to Dori Ganan and Leslie Corral, who own a pet supply store and adoption resource center. Dori is the partner with the penchant for animals, and Leslie has the business head. Dori's love for animals came out strongly when she lived in California, just down the street from the local animal shelter. She visited it at least five times a week and adopted her first three pets there—two dogs and one cat. Once she got them home, her desire to give them the best possible life began. Walking with her pets and friends always took a long time because she stopped to talk to every other pet owner along the way.

Dori began to prepare for her career with animals when she took a course in dog grooming. But that wasn't for her, so she went to work as a dog walker. That's when she and Leslie decided to start their own dog-walking service. But Dori's short-lived experience as a groomer taught her about dog and cat body language and how to read them. She has always had a huge interest in animal health and has read natural healing books on both dogs and cats, which is really her main interest.

Neither Dori nor Leslie had any professional training on how to run a business, but they read many books on the subject. They learned a lot over the years, often by making mistakes. Leslie is taking a marketing class now, and when she is finished, Dori is going to take a computer class.

They would recommend that anyone who might want to start a business like theirs take a business course. They believe that learning negotiation skills, for example, might have saved them some money along the way had they taken a few courses. Some small businesses also offer consulting services for a fee.

Dori and Leslie have also found a great deal of business information on the Internet that they wished had been there when they started out. Belonging to your local chamber of commerce and to industry-related professional organizations can also be helpful.

They do know that good customer service is what most people want. Because they run a small neighborhood shop, they get to know their customers and their preferences very well. They know that if they don't care about the customers and their pets, those customers will find somewhere else to shop. Dori and Leslie want their customers to tell their friends about the great service they receive at their store.

The greatest reward for them is helping customers find solutions for the many problems pets may have. Maybe the pet has allergies or needs a special diet. If their products help the pet to improve, they have a happy customer forever—and that's what they aim for with everyone who comes through their door.

Store owners should also keep in touch with local groomers, trainers, veterinarians, and breeders. It's a good idea to attend pet shows, read trade publications, and keep up with trends in nutrition, play needs, and new products. Attending business seminars or classes is also very helpful. But the primary characteristic of a successful pet supply store owner is a love of animals and an understanding of owners. Getting to know both pets and owners and accommodating your business to them should be your major concern.

Pet Groomers

A neighborhood business that involves much direct contact with animals is that of a pet groomer. Some groomers also operate boarding kennels, and others sell pet care products. A much smaller number also breed and train animals. Most groomers handle dogs only, while a small number groom cats. Usually groomers have to work full-time. The typical grooming shop has two to three employees, often family members.

According to a recent survey, the majority of groomers went into business because of their love of animals. But groomers also must enjoy working with people because groomers deal directly with pet owners. Groomers are needed in both small towns and big cities and can earn high salaries, depending on their locations.

How to Become a Groomer

Groomers approach their careers in one of three ways: by serving an apprenticeship under an experienced groomer, by attending a trade school, or by teaching themselves. Most participate in training programs throughout their careers and continue to read trade journals. Others may also attend seminars and classes. Some groomers who own their own shops may provide ongoing training for their employees. They also may attend professional conventions and trade shows.

A Typical Day as a Groomer

Specific services provided at most grooming operations include nail clipping, cleaning ears and teeth, bathing, dipping, hot-oil treatments, brushing, combing, styling, and clipping and trimming coats. The customer may opt for individual services or a complete grooming for a set fee. Nail clipping is often considered a separate service.

Most groomers separate the cats from the dogs. Groomers should also share any potential health problems an animal may have so that the owner can report them to the vet.

Products that groomers sell include collars, flea-control treatments, food, clothes, and beds. They may also sell grooming supplies, such as shampoo, brushes, and combs. If you decide to board animals in addition to providing grooming services, you will have to provide cages and runs. You should also plan on summer being your busiest season for boarding.

In addition to hiring other groomers, a shop owner may have a veterinarian on call, an accountant to handle the books, a lawyer to consult about contracts and liability, and an insurance agent. Most shop owners handle their own publicity, which may consist simply of a display ad in the yellow pages of the local telephone directory. Word-of-mouth advertising is always very effective, with radio, television, direct mail, newspapers, the Internet, and billboards being other possibilities.

As is the case with all people who choose to work directly with animals, groomers often work long hours and have to deal with large animals on a daily basis. Grooming shop owners must sometimes be on call. They also must deal with a host of other problems to be solved and decisions to be made. For example, as an owner, you might have trouble finding competent and reliable employees, and you also need to carefully select a location that will be attractive to customers.

Education and Employment Outlook

As with animal trainers, there are no real educational standards or licensing procedures for pet groomers. The National Dog Groomers Association of America is a professional organization that offers workshops and certification tests to all of its members.

Through such organizations, members can network and attend conventions, seminars, and competitions. If you choose to apprentice with an experienced groomer, be sure to check that groomer's credentials and reputation.

Many groomers feel that the lack of professional status prevents them from charging fees that are commensurate with their work and skills. As a business owner, you set your own fees, but they need to be based on what you can reasonably expect to charge in your local market. Check fees that are prevalent in your area and charge accordingly.

Animals need regular grooming to maintain their appearance and good health. No matter what part of the country you live in, your services as a groomer will be in demand for owners who lack the time or skill to groom their own animals. There can be a good future for you as a groomer, but before you commit yourself to this career, talk to groomers and volunteer at grooming facilities to gain enough experience to know whether this career choice is the right one for you.

Custom-Made Products for Pets

Some enterprising pet fanciers make a good living by producing or selling items that appeal to other animal lovers. Whether you make bird houses, cat toys, or dog beds, or just have a knack for knowing what kinds of products will sell, you can find sales outlets through online stores, mail-order catalogs, pet shows, craft fairs, and pet supply stores.

Mail-Order Businesses

The possibilities are almost unlimited for mail-order businesses related to animals. Besides the usual collars, leashes, toys, and flea products, pet supply catalogs and websites offer books about almost any animal, pet memorials, natural and gourmet pet foods, dog-food cookbooks, dog houses, animal rubber stamps and note cards, pet tags, animal hood ornaments for your car, and bandanas in various designs for your dog. Cut-crystal pet dishes, cedar-log dog houses, pet doors, and programmable food dispensers are also sold via mail order.

Cat furniture and accessories that match the owner's own décor are also available. Often custom designed, these ensembles are geared to owners who may be a bit fussy about cluttering up their homes with ordinary pet accessories. One TV commercial specializes in pet stairs for cats and dogs who cannot jump because of injury, old age, surgery, or arthritis.

Many animal-related subjects are now available on cassette or videotape and can be sent through the mail. Some tapes specialize in training, others in grooming. One videotape may feature dogs of all kinds—just dogs! Another videotape may demonstrate nature photography, and another might show birds, squirrels, and other wild animals scampering in their natural habitats to amuse the indoor cat in your life. Other possibilities for mail-order products include coffee mugs and T-shirts with animal imprints, personalized checks with animal pictures, pet diapers, and designer pet clothes.

The advent of e-tailing—retail shops doing business over the Internet—has opened a whole new range of opportunities for the enterprising animal lover. Products that can be sold in a shop or through the mail can also be sold over the Internet.

A Cat House Architect

Healthy pets need an environment that both provides amusement and fulfills their basic needs. For example, cats have a real need to climb, jump, nap, scratch, play, and feel sheltered—and they like to do all that in a place they can call their own.

Enter George Ney—again. We met him earlier in his role as a cat trainer. But before he began training and showing cats, his imagination and love of felines led him to create elaborate cat houses, condominiums, scratching posts, duplexes, castles, perches, and race cars—almost any kind of digs that cats would love.

Each creation always has at least one tree limb incorporated into it because trees are cats' natural scratching posts. George used to sell carpeting, so he had a lot of carpet overstock on hand to cover the posts and perches.

Observing cats long enough will tell you that they love comfort, security, and heights. George capitalized on his knowledge of cats' needs and his knowledge of carpentry. Starting out simply with spools, he then built taller and more elaborate houses with different sizes and shapes of perches, platforms, and tubes. Most kittens stay in the lower parts of a more elaborate house until they are big enough to climb or jump to the top. George's cat condos and other furniture were so attractive to cats and owners alike that he was able to make his living selling them.

George's designs for the houses and furniture are limited only by his imagination. He uses tree limbs, tubing, a staple gun, glue, plywood, and carpeting—all materials that are easy to acquire— to make fantastic creations.

George builds his houses with the help of a designer and an assistant at his shop. He sets his own prices according to the labor and materials involved. He also wrote a book to teach others how to build their own cat condos or creations in whatever form they choose.

Pet Sitters

A comparatively new industry, pet sitting, is now emerging, due in large part to the fact that most American households have pets, and many of these households have two incomes and no children. When these pet owners must travel for business or work too many long hours, they want their pets to receive good care and attention. Some households with pets consist of elderly or infirm people for whom the pet is therapeutic. And although the owners may not be able to fully take care of their pets, they don't want to give them up. The pet-sitting business is custom-made for these households.

Pet sitting differs from operating a boarding kennel because the sitter actually takes care of the pet in the pet's own home. This arrangement provides security for the pet and convenience for the owner. The pet is also spared any illness that it might pick up at a boarding kennel or animal shelter.

In addition, many pet sitters provide other services, especially for the owners who are on vacation. These services include watering plants, bringing in the mail, and turning lights on and off, which may deter burglars from breaking in while the owners are away.

Flexible Possibilities for Pet Sitters

Pet sitting can provide you with a flexible career, if you're so inclined. Pet sitting can be an additional service provided by a pet supply shop owner, a full- or part-time career, or just a seasonal occupation. You can run the business out of an existing pet store or from your home. You can have a large staff or run your business as a one-person operation. Because the peak vacation period is usually during the summer, you may decide to confine your services to that time. Or you may want to work year-round, including weekends and holidays. Homemakers, teachers, retired people, or people temporarily out of work may want to put a few hours a week into pet sitting.

Becoming a Professional Pet Sitter

If you plan to start your own pet-sitting business, you should love animals, of course, but there are no real educational or training prerequisites. A business background would be helpful, but common sense combined with a sense of humor can take you a long way. And remember that the term *pet* may include not only cats and dogs, but also hamsters, rabbits, gerbils, turtles, and snakes!

If you run a home-based operation, your initial investment will be minimal. Because you go to the pets' homes, you need only a telephone (and perhaps a separate business line), an answering machine, a computer, basic office supplies, business cards and/or fliers, and liability insurance. If you run your business from a pet store, you need only add on the service to the others that you provide. Grooming and boarding businesses also may add pet sitting to their basic services.

Successful pet sitters might offer you the following advice: Be sure to get liability insurance and have all employees bonded and insured. Have a service contract specifying all the services that the owner wants performed, in addition to the pet's dietary requirements and necessary medicine. Obtain from the owner emergency phone numbers, veterinarian's number, list of toys the pet plays with, and required grooming.

Before you sign any contract, however, set up a meeting with the pet's owner in the owner's home so that you can meet the pet and get to know its habits and environment. At the same time, you can determine whether the pet is a biter or generally too dangerous or rowdy to take on as a client.

Because each owner has different requirements, the amount of time that you spend with each pet will vary. The pets' personalities will all be different, which is an attractive feature of this career— variety. But if you have steady customers and more than one employee, it is a good idea to send the same sitter to the same customer to establish continuity for the animal.

As an independent contractor, you will be able to set your own rates. The National Association of Pet Sitters recommends per diem rates. Your rates may vary according to your location, with higher rates being paid in larger cities. Any additional services unrelated to pet sitting, such as picking up the owner's dry cleaning, would be charged separately. Most sitters require a down payment of some kind.

If you have your own business with employees, you must train them thoroughly and make sure that they are responsible. Having irresponsible or unreliable employees would be a major drawback in this business—most owners feel that their pet is part of the family and want it treated accordingly.

You will also need to consider advertising your service. Because there are so many pets on every street in the country, there is most likely a need for pet sitting in your location. You can advertise at cat and dog shows, with breeders and groomers, and through local veterinarians and pet shops.

More Businesses Built Around Animals

Financial Management for Animal Welfare

If you are used to dealing with financial matters, you might consider managing investment portfolios for animal welfare organizations, such as humane shelters, which often have certain ethical standards about how their money should be invested. Pet health insurance is also an up-and-coming business to get into. Some banks offer credit cards to pet owners who also receive an optional pet health insurance package as well as discount coupons for pet food and supplies.

Dog Camp

Camps for dogs and their owners offer individualized training in obedience and agility for the dogs. Guest lecturers cover such subjects as agility, breed handling, first aid, therapy, and fieldwork. The owners have the opportunity to swim, walk, and relax.

Adoption Centers

Some working and racing dogs, such as greyhounds, can be rescued from death by adoption centers after their racing careers have ended. These centers specialize in training these dogs to be pets. The grateful dogs need, in the meantime, only to be boarded and cared for while waiting for adoption. This may not be a paying occupation, but experience with such an organization can lead to other paid employment.

Pet Theft Prevention

Some businesspeople are concerned with the theft or loss of your pet. Just as your DVD player can be stolen and sold for cash, so can your dog or cat. Stolen pets are often sold to laboratories for experimentation. Certain companies help to track down lost or stolen pets by tattooing and registering them.

Recent advances in microchip technology have spawned a new industry in animal protection. A tiny microchip with a unique number embedded on it is inserted under an animal's skin, and that pet identification number is registered on a national database along with the owner's information. Animal shelters and veterinary hospitals have scanners that can read these microchips and match the animals with their owners.

Other entrepreneurs supply concerned pet owners with directories of overnight lodgings that accept pets, so that pets can travel along with their owners.

Cruelty-Free Personal Care Suppliers

There are some entrepreneurial businesses run by animal lovers, such as Anita Roddick's the Body Shop, that specialize in supplying products that are free of all animal ingredients or byproducts or that were developed without experimentation on animals. Products available through such companies include cosmetics, hair-care products, bubble bath and bath oil, skin-care products, household cleaners, and baby products. Because more and more consumers are choosing not to wear leather, a business can offer nonleather shoes, purses, wallets, and briefcases. Vegetarian cookbooks, T-shirts, and sweatshirts are also available.

No More Dissections

Also available through similar organizations are classroom devices that reduce or eliminate the need to dissect frogs or fetal pigs, as has been the practice in biology classes for years. A computer simulation for grade-school students is available that shows the youngsters which instruments would be used in dissection and how to locate and remove specific organs and magnify them for observation. The program allows for diagrams and animation. Then the students can "reconstruct" the frog and see him as he hops away—all this without a live animal!

Veterinarian colleges can use electronic mannequins of cats and dogs to reduce the number of live animals used for certain training techniques. These dummies have pulses, fur, teeth, and plastic organs. They can be used to help budding veterinarians develop the correct touching techniques for animals of different size and weight. If too much pressure is applied, a light goes on and the student tries again. Films are now available to show symptoms of animal illness and operating and treatment techniques to cut down on the use of real animals in the operating room. For more information on organizations concerned with the humane treatment of animals, see Chapter 9.

Green Pet Care

Other entrepreneurs are becoming more aware of potentially harmful ingredients in commercial pet food and flea-control products—thus, a natural pet foods and products industry is emerging. Flea collars and shampoos, combs, and herbal powders are now for sale as well as natural remedies for arthritic pets. Other businesspeople supply natural, chemical-free food and treats for pets.

Pet Transport

A small but growing field is the pet transport business, which usually entails bringing the pet to or from the airport when the pet's plane arrives before the owner's flight. Pet transporters also may provide basic taxi service for pets, taking them to the veterinarian or the groomer. No formal education or training is necessary to be a pet transporter, although this profession does have a professional organization, the Independent Pet and Animal Transportation Association.

The need for this service exists in most communities, but it may not be large enough to serve as your sole source of income. For that reason, some pet transporters are also pet shop owners or kennel operators. To get into the business, you need first a love of animals and a van or truck. If your business is successful you can expand, hire employees, and send out more vans. For transporting larger animals, such as horses, you would need an appropriate trailer equipped for the animals' safety.

Having boarding facilities can boost your pet transport business, especially with customers who are moving to your city. They may want to send their pet along beforehand and need someone to both pick up the pet and board it until they arrive. As a pet transporter and boarder, you need to be on call twenty-four hours a day, year-round. Your employees must be reliable, dependable, and lovers of animals. They must also be good drivers and know their way around your city.

Pet Breeders

You may decide that you would like to have direct contact with only one kind of animal and specialize in breeding German shepherds or Russian blues or Scottish folds, for example. This career requires preparation, either by apprenticing under an experienced groomer or by taking college courses in genetics and animal health care. Standards for this career are set by the National Pet Dealers and Breeders Association.

As a breeder, your work consists of planning matings and exhibiting the animals at shows. You also feed, groom, and clean the animals and help them through pregnancy, delivery, and raising their young. You should have close contact with a veterinarian, maintain health and genealogical records, and find potential buyers.

Pet Cemeteries

Pets get old and die just like humans, and many owners choose to bury their pets in a cemetery or have them cremated. If pets are buried, they need a stone or marker. Some pets are buried in specially designed caskets.

The International Association of Pet Cemeteries and Crematories is the professional association that sets the standards and regulations for members who are owners of cemeteries and crematories. Its aim is to upgrade the industry and to assure pet owners of a resting place for their companion animals. If members adhere to the basic standards established by the association, their facilities are designated as approved pet cemeterics. The membership association provides continuous education, management consultation, public recognition, and promotional materials.

Starting a Business That Focuses on Animals

As you can see, in starting a pet-related business, you can fill an already established need by becoming a pet supply store owner or kennel operator, or you can let your imagination run free and build cat condos or sell gourmet pet food and recipes. Because there are so many pets in this country, there are also concerned pet owners who are willing to pay for quality nutrition and care for their faithful companions. Also, pet owners generally like to own animal-related objects, such as mugs, note cards, playing cards, T-shirts, and sweatshirts. These all have to be provided by businesspeople. Pet-related business ideas are limited only by the entrepreneur's imagination and the needs of pets and their owners.

Some businesses require little or no formal education or training, but they do require careful observation, common sense, business acumen, love of animals, courage, and a sense of humor. Affiliation with a professional association related to your business interest will be most helpful in getting your business started.

People in pet-related businesses often know each other and will cooperate with advertising and referrals if you have a good reputation. If no formal training is available in your area, it is always helpful to talk to other people in the business, go to pet shows, work part-time, and volunteer. Apprentice under the best person in the community so that your reputation will gain credibility.

You may eventually combine businesses, such as those of kennel operator and pet transporter, cat trainer and furniture maker, groomer and pet sitter. Keep up with new trends in technology and medical treatment of animals. Talk to veterinarians about physiological needs of animals or to therapists about psychological needs. Read trade publications, especially the advertisements, to see where you might apply your natural animal-loving instincts. Contact professional associations for membership requirements and standards. They can often supply you with reading lists and educational requirements, as well as provide social networking possibilities.

Is a Pet-Related Business Right for You?

You should also carefully assess your own personal talents and inclinations. You should ask yourself if you want to work directly with animals, whether you want to own your own business or work for someone else, how much money you want to earn, and how much time and money you want to invest in your career.

You may prefer to work in an office preparing investment portfolios for animal-related organizations. Or your business background may have prepared you for the lucrative mail-order or Internet industries, where you can either provide for the needs of the animals or the whimsies of the owners. You may have been deeply affected at one time or another by the prolonged illness and death of a pet and choose to specialize in the design and manufacture of equipment that will relieve pain, suffering, or disability of animals, or you may even decide to open a pet cemetery or crematory.

Ask yourself some questions that may help you make up your mind about the type of business that would interest you:

1. Am I more comfortable working in an office with regular hours and a steady income?
2. Do my background and training involve business courses rather than animal-related courses?
3. Do I like to keep records, make appointments, and schedule assignments for employees?
4. Does my talent lie in administration rather than fieldwork?
5. Do I love to work with animals of any kind, at any time, anywhere?
6. Do I enjoy trying to explain to an owner what I'm doing and why?
7. Am I prepared to deal with the more unpleasant parts of the job, such as illness and death of an animal?
8. Am I able to do strenuous work with irregular hours?

If you answered yes to the first four questions, you are probably better suited to owning a pet shop, running a mail-order or Internet business, being a pet supplier, or selling animal-related products. If you answered yes to the last four questions, you might be ready for an active career as a groomer, kennel operator, pet sitter, or transporter.

If you can combine people and pet skills, your business possibilities are almost unlimited. You may want to work for professional organizations and help set standards for others in the field. Or you may want to establish an organization for your line of work if one doesn't already exist.

If you have an idea, a talent, a cause, a love for animals, an understanding of the human/animal relationship, a natural curiosity, a need to share, abundant energy and patience, common sense, and a sense of humor, you can have a career in an animal-related business. It's really up to you. The animals and their owners are waiting.

For More Information

Publications

Clark, A.J. *Animal Breeding: Technology for the 21st Century*. Harwood Academic Publishers, 1998.

Moran, Patti J. *Pet Sitting for Profit: A Complete Manual for Success*. New Beginnings, 1998.

Roth, Suzanne. *The Reality of Professional Pet Sitting*. Xlibris, 1999.

Associations

American Boarding Kennels Association and American
    Grooming Shop Association
1702 East Pikes Peak Avenue
Colorado Springs, CO 80909
www.abka.com

Animal Transportation Association
111 East Loop North
Houston, TX 77029
www.aata-animaltransport.org

Independent Pet and Animal Transportation Association
745 Winding Trail
Holly Lake Ranch, TX 75755
www.ipata.com

International Association of Pet Cemeteries and Crematories
  (IAOPCC)
PO Box 163
5055 Route 11
Ellenburg Depot, NY 12935
www.iaopc.com

International Professional Groomers
120 Turner Avenue
Elk Grove Village, IL 60007
www.ipgcmg.org

National Association of Professional Pet Sitters (NAPPS)
15000 Commerce Parkway, Suite C
Mt. Laurel, NJ 08054
www.petsitters.org

Pet Sitters International (PSI)
201 East King Street
King, NC 27021
www.petsit.com

World Wide Pet Industry Association (WWPIA)
406 South First Avenue
Arcadia, CA 91006
www.wwpia.org

CHAPTER SIX

Telling Their Stories, Reflecting Their Beauty

Some people base their animal-related careers on their creative talents. They include artists, designers, musicians, photographers, writers, illustrators, and filmmakers and videographers. Others make it possible for creative people to display their talents, such as book and magazine publishers, museum curators, gallery owners, website designers, and professional organizations.

Writing and Publishing Books About Animals

If you open a catalog from any bookseller, log on to the Internet, or go to any bookstore, you will find a wide variety of books about animals. Some are fictitious; some are based on real-life experiences. Some are about domesticated animals; others are about farm or wild animals. Still others are on training, grooming, and care of animals. Others cover one breed of dog, cat, or horse.

A growing number of books are concerned with animal rights, animal behavior patterns, and animal pathology. Some are geared toward adults; others are for children. Some are primarily used as textbooks for veterinary schools. Others are about specific career tracks with animals.

For every book published, there is a writer, editor, artist, designer, and photographer or illustrator. All of these creative people collaborate on books about dog astrology, obedience training or training in police work, naming your animal, jogging with your dog, or showing your pet.

Becoming a Writer

A real writer, it could be said, can write about any topic, but a true love of animals might compel you to write exclusively about them. All writers must have very specific skills that, though rooted in creativity, are generally honed with academic courses such as grammar, spelling, vocabulary building, research, and composition. In addition to these skills, a writer has to be able to tell a story, describe a process, or factually detail a character or situation in words. Writers who work for a trade magazine or newspaper should also possess interviewing skills and the ability to meet deadlines.

Making Some Choices

If you possess these skills, you need to decide on your career aim, such as whether you want to write books or articles for magazines or newspapers. You may also be interested in writing scripts for films and videotapes about some phase of animal life.

The requirements for all writing jobs are essentially the same as far as language skills are concerned, and these skills must be highly developed. Knowledge of the subject and a firm grasp of technical vocabulary are often necessary, which may mean further study, either formally or informally.

Writers also may decide to specialize in a particular animal or breed and, if so, which aspect, angle, or approach to cover. Then they may choose between writing for children or adults. If you decide to write animal stories for children, you should be familiar with age-appropriate language and subject matter.

Another choice is whether to write fact or fiction. Fiction writers invent unique animals in unusual circumstances; other writers tell of real animal heroes rescuing people and saving lives. Some nonfiction writers are veterinarians, trainers, breeders, scientists, or animal behaviorists who are experts in their fields and who share their knowledge with the general public.

If you decide upon factual writing, your research skills will be very useful, in addition to your powers of observation, curiosity about various topics or subject matters, and ability to organize the results of your research into a coherent presentation. Your purpose will be to inform or educate.

If you decide to specialize in animal fiction, research skills and mastery of grammar are also necessary, but your research may focus more on background material to support your soaring imagination and ability to create new characters in the context of a story line. The purpose of fiction is more to entertain than to educate, so humor, irony, metaphor, descriptions, and emotions (such as fear, sorrow, love, and anger) will enhance your narrative. The ability to conjure animal characters with distinctive characteristics is also essential to the animal fiction writer's craft.

Textbook writers should be experts in the field but will also need to establish the scope of the book, organize a vast amount of material into a teachable whole, and be thorough and accurate in presentation. Depending on the level of readership, the textbook writer must also use appropriate vocabulary and terminology.

More Options for Writers

In addition to writing about animals for magazine editors and book publishers, here are some other choices to consider.

Public Relations Writers. Humane societies, professional organizations, small businesses, corporations, and governmental agencies that deal with animals produce information packets, pamphlets, brochures, and descriptive literature to disseminate information and educate the public. Sometimes these organizations employ a full-time staff of writers, or they may hire freelance writers.

Book Editors. Every writer hopes to have a good editor, one who knows even more about the mechanics of the language, has superb spelling skills, knows and understands the subject matter, has a coherent and organized mind, and does not hesitate to improve the manuscript. For fiction, an editor also needs to be able to feel the emotions evoked by the author and respond to them. Editors have to work well with a variety of people including the author, designer, copyeditor, illustrator, proofreader, or typesetter.

Creating Animal Illustrations

Illustrators, artists, and designers are needed for books, encyclopedias, pamphlets, movies, brochures, websites, and medical charts. Medical or scientific illustrators must be able to draw the anatomy and physiology of many different animals realistically and accurately.

Others may invent stylized versions or whimsical imaginings of animals for works of fiction or animated movies, cartoons, or greeting cards. These may be instructional pieces or solely for the purpose of entertaining.

Computer artists can create remarkably accurate simulations of animals for demonstrating treatments and operating techniques for animal health care.

Fine artists may specialize in either domesticated, wild, or farm animals. If they choose to do realistic studies of particular animals or birds, either for books, portraits, or calendars, they need considerable artistic skill in addition to detailed knowledge of the animal's anatomy, coloring, habitat, proportions, and dimensions. For example, a wildlife artist may want to capture the exciting physical appearance of an eagle about to descend on its prey.

Pet portrait artists, on the other hand, may want to learn more about a particular pet's personality, activities, and relationship to its owner in order to capture the animal on canvas. Some people have unusual pets, such as rabbits, ferrets, horses, snakes, tarantulas, and pigs, and pet portraitists paint them, too. Sometimes a pet portraitist is commissioned to be the official painter at an exhibition or competition. Pet portraitists work in a variety of mediums, including oils, acrylics, watercolors, pastels, charcoal, and ink. Some photographers also specialize in pet portraits.

The possibilities for further opportunities unfold if you keep up on trends, read trade publications, and stay current with upcoming events.

A Pet Portraitist

Kay Alport, a pet portraitist, specializes in dogs and cats. She has successfully combined her creative talent with her love of animals. She began studying art as a girl and majored in fine arts in college. After that, she was a successful fashion illustrator for major retail stores, both as an employee and as a freelance illustrator.

Much of the market for fashion illustrators has, however, dissolved in the past several years. Several major retailers closed down during that time, and others were bought up by companies with corporate headquarters elsewhere. Kay's freelance work began to disappear.

But creative people often adapt to adversity by turning their talents in other directions. So Kay took her experience with oil painting and her love of dogs and explored the possibility of pet portraiture. She feared, though, that nobody would like her work, so she started out by painting a portrait of a favorite dog as a gift for a friend, Jim Morgan, her dog's trainer. Jim liked the painting so much that Kay started painting portraits of certain breeds, although she didn't yet feel secure enough to enter the field of personalized pet portraiture as a career.

But Jim displayed her paintings at his training facility, and Kay started advertising her craft in national trade publications. She went to pet shows, and Jim kept exhibiting her paintings. Then Kay advertised in local publications, which was less expensive than advertising nationally, and the customers started coming in. Kay also says that dog owners are easier to find than cat owners because dogs must be taken out for walks. Sometimes these walks turn into networking sessions for Kay and her neighbors.

The Creative Process. When potential customers are interested in having their pets portrayed in oil, they send Kay a good photograph of the animal, or more than one, if a particular setting or background would depict the pet more naturally. At that time, they specify whether they want a full-face or full-body portrait. Kay has samples of different backgrounds for the owners to choose from.

The customer pays a nonrefundable deposit. Kay says it may take her from two days to two weeks to achieve the kind of portrait she wants. She then sends a photo of the almost finished portrait to the owner. At that time, the owner can phone or write in any changes to Kay. When all is agreed upon, Kay frames the painting, includes the nail and hook, and ships the painting to clients all over the country. Many of these customers become friends because of Kay's personalized treatment of their beloved companion animals, even though Kay worked from a photo. Kay has also developed a line of note cards with pen-and-ink sketches of pets. She sells the cards with envelopes in boxes of 50, 100, or 150. She also arranges for gift certificates to be sent to family or friends on special occasions.

Although Kay was in advertising for years, she says that the most difficult part of her job is self-promotion. She was well accustomed to telling potential customers how wonderful someone else's products or services were, but it's another story when it comes to saying good things about herself. In most cases, though, her work speaks for itself, and her clients are always satisfied. Publicity and promotion are vital parts of an entrepreneur's existence, so brochures, fliers, and business cards must appeal to pet owners and be displayed in the places where dog and cat owners will see them. Kay has a permanent exhibit at Jim Morgan's, and a good deal of her publicity comes from satisfied customers. Advertising in local newspapers also brings in business.

In her studio, which has representations of animals in one form or another all around her easel, Kay enjoys the best part of the job—painting. Kay can envision herself painting cats and dogs for the rest of her life and looks forward to it.

Photographing Wildlife

Wildlife photographers are in demand for books, videotapes, movies, and television shows. Individual photographs can be exhibited at art galleries and museums or published in books or periodicals. Pictures of animals, including birds, fish, and reptiles in their natural habitats, are needed to realistically portray behavior patterns, socialization, and foraging in textbooks. These are usually informative and educational in nature and often relate to the total environment.

Pictures of domesticated animals may be used to illustrate grooming and training techniques, breed characteristics, anatomy, health care, and surgical techniques. Pictures of racehorses and horse races are not only attractive but demonstrate winning characteristics. In fact, photos have often determined which horse won a close race. Working around horses at horse farms or stables and talking with trainers and owners will give you a feel for the animals and enhance your photos.

Photographers of wild animals must become familiar with the animals' social habits, behavioral patterns, feeding routines, and care of their young. Knowledge of predator-prey relationships will be helpful in stalking the animal for action shots.

Some wildlife photographers have branched out from taking pictures to producing video workshops on nature photography.

These videos can be geared for the beginner or the professional and may share tips on exposure, composition, close-ups, and marketing. Other photographers conduct wildlife photography trips to national parks in the United States and photo safaris in Africa and other parts of the world. Some expeditions may be geared toward gathering specific photos for particular publications, such as magazines, trade publications, or books.

Exhibiting in Museums and Galleries

Some creative people opt to work in natural history museums, where they are responsible for researching and setting up exhibits relating to specific animals and birds. These exhibits are largely educational and informative in intent but can be quite creative in execution and appearance.

Still other creative people own or are employed at art galleries that exhibit the best in regional, national, or international painters, photographers, or illustrators of animals. These are the people who can spot talent in someone else but who prefer to remain in the background to showcase that talent. As a gallery owner or operator, you would be concerned more with scheduling and setting up exhibits, transporting the artwork, publicizing the exhibits, and handling administration. Through sales of art, you make it possible for painters and photographers to make a living with their talents.

Starting Your Creative Career

Whichever career path you choose to take, you will have to combine both creative and technical skills. It is not enough just to have ideas—you must be able to translate those ideas into a sentence, an image, a photo, or a painting. Each process requires different talents.

Education and Training

Writers, editors, artists, illustrators, and photographers, therefore, must have formal training in their crafts. Writers and editors must know what makes a good sentence and how to use sentences to form paragraphs; they also need to be skilled in the use of a computer. Artists and illustrators must know how to select and use paintbrushes, pastels, oils, or watercolors; how to combine colors; how to create perspective; and how to portray animal activities, qualities, and personalities. Photographers must know how to operate a film or video camera; which lens to use; how to use lighting; and how to compose the best picture according to light, exposure, and purpose.

Most creative careers require a college degree—whether in English, creative writing, journalism, graphic design, photography, or fine arts—or at least formal instruction in writing composition, photography, art, or design. Further education might entail attending workshops and seminars, reading trade publications, networking with others in the field, attending exhibitions, and entering into competitions with other professionals.

Writers should read and write about animals in any context, just to develop writing skills and to learn more about animals. Artists should draw or paint regularly even if they are between assignments, and photographers should always have a camera on hand—you never know when the perfect photo opportunity will occur. If you are multitalented, you may be able to combine writing and photography or illustrating. But the necessary technical skills must be learned before any of your creative ideas can move on to paper, canvas, film, or tape.

Making Career Choices

If you choose any of these creative careers relating to animals, you may opt to work as an employee on a full-time basis or as an independent contractor. If you are employed full-time, you will receive a steady salary and benefits, including insurance, paid vacations, and sick days. You may even receive a pension plan or tuition reimbursement to further your education.

However, if you choose to work independently, as many creative people do, you run the risk of not having work during certain periods of the year. You will also need to pay for your own insurance and supplies and be responsible for your own advertising, promotion, and publicity.

Each choice has decided advantages and disadvantages—you will make the decision according to your own temperament and financial requirements. If you can exist with little or no income for certain times during the year but love to work by yourself at your own pace, freelance work may be for you. If, on the other hand, you like working with other people for a set number of hours a day, being employed by an organization should suit you.

Or you may start out with an organization and eventually become independent. For example, you may begin by illustrating books for a publishing company and then branch off on your own, after you have saved up some money and built a good reputation in your field. By this time, you may even have fostered a clientele who will supply you with work.

Selling Your Work

As a writer, artist, or photographer who works on your own, you must generate your own ideas, which then have to be sold to book, magazine, or newspaper publishers; to video or film producers; or to art galleries or museums. This will entail some research on your part to see what has been done on the topic you want to cover. Your angle or approach or particular specialty may be just what the publisher or producer is looking for.

If you want to submit your idea to a magazine, determine whether it has recently published an article on that topic. If so, you will want to submit the idea to another publisher. Or you may want to expand your idea to develop a book-length manuscript on the topic. Then check to see which book publishers specialize in your particular field. Browse through bookstores, libraries, and magazine stands to get a good idea of what has already been published.

You can also check your local zoo, aquarium, humane society, or any of the national humane education, animal welfare, or animal rights organizations to see if they need writers, photographers, or illustrators for their information kits, press releases and packets, pamphlets, and brochures. Many of these groups, especially the national organizations, publish many materials each year and use large numbers of freelancers in addition to the talented people they have on staff.

Textbook publishers always need writers or illustrators to hire on a full-time or freelance basis. These books are usually technical and realistic in nature, so you may need a background in medical terminology or drawing to qualify.

Professional societies that specialize in a particular species or breed may publish their own magazines. If you have an idea for a videotape about animals, you can submit your proposal to a producer for review and possible approval. Videotapes require the combined work of writers, artists, illustrators, and videographers.

And for each business that produces T-shirts, sweatshirts, coffee mugs, note cards, key chains, calendars, bank checks, greeting cards, scarves, belt buckles, watches, clocks, or baby products with animal pictures on them, an artist is needed. Advertising copy has to be written for these products, and the ads need designers and illustrators.

Outlook and Earnings

Career opportunities for writers and editors, either self-employed or employed by a company, look good through 2012, with the best opportunities for technical writers or specialists. Salaried writers had a median income of around $44,350 in 2004. For editors, it was $43,890. Freelance writers and editors can set their terms according to their local markets, usually higher in large cities.

Artists in general have a favorable outlook through 2012. Median earnings for salaried fine artists and illustrators were $38,060 in 2004; for multimedia artists and animators, $50,360. Self-employed artists charge according to experience, reputation, and location.

Photographers employed by a company earned a median annual salary of $26,000 in 2004. Those working for newspapers and magazines had median annual earnings of $32,000, and $23,100 was the median for other professionals. Photographers face keen competition, especially for salaried jobs. Salaried photographers tend to earn more than freelancers.

A Wide Open Field

Because there are so many pets in this country, pet-related businesses are booming. With the added emphasis now on protecting the environment and preserving species, much of the focus has turned to wildlife and its preservation. So the market for animal-loving creative people is nearly unlimited. Pet owners never seem to tire of reading about or viewing pictures of their own or others' pets or exemplars of their favorite breeds.

Armed with your creative ability and technical skills, along with a little business savvy, you should be able to combine your talents for a long and happy career. Joining a professional organization and networking with other people in animal-related businesses will help with promoting and publicizing your business. Reading trade publications and attending shows will help you focus on your market and clientele.

You may decide to work full-time for an established publisher, videotape producer, greeting card company, or animal-related organization. Or you may be so creative that you create a brand-new career, never before thought of. If a need is there, you will fill it. The field is truly wide open, and new possibilities arise every day for those who are alert, aware, and attentive. Changes in technology and taste, as well as shifts in the needs of society and animals, can put you on the creative edge of a long and happy career.

For More Information

Publications

Brewer, Robert Lee, ed. *Writer's Market*. Writer's Digest Books, annual.

Cox, Mary, ed. *Artist's and Graphic Designer's Market*. Writer's Digest Books, annual.

Drochon, Christophe, and Françoise Coffrant. *Painting Animals*. New Holland, 2006.

Fleishman, Michael. *Starting Your Career as a Freelance Illustrator or Graphic Designer*. Allworth Press, 2001.

Muska, Debrah H. *Professional Techniques for Pet and Animal Photography*. Amherst Media, 2003.

Poehner, Donna, and Erika O'Connell. *Photographer's Market*. Writer's Digest Books, annual.

Pope, Alice, ed. *Children's Writer's and Illustrator's Market*. Writer's Digest Books, annual.

Scott, Jeanne Filler. *Painting Animal Friends*. North Light Books, 2005.

Silber, Lee. *Self-Promotion for the Creative Person: Get the Word Out About Who You Are and What You Do*. Three Rivers Press, 2001.

Associations

American Society of Magazine Editors
Magazine Publishers of America
810 Seventh Avenue, Twenty-Fourth Floor
New York, NY 10019
www.magazine.org

American Society of Photographers
PO Box 1120
Caldwell, TX 77836
www.asofp-online.com

The Dog Writers' Association of America
173 Union Road
Coatesville, PA 19320
www.dwaa.org

Graphic Arts Guild
90 John Street, Suite 403
New York, NY 10038
www.gag.org

Outdoor Writers Association of America
121 Hickory Streer, Suite 1
Missoula, MT 59801
www.owaa.org

Professional Photographers of America
229 Peachtree Street, Suite 2200
Atlanta, GA 30303
www.ppa.com

CHAPTER SEVEN

Working with Exotic Animals

Everyone has been to the zoo, wildlife park, or aquarium at one time or another, and many have made a return trip with their children or grandchildren. In North America alone, millions of people visit zoological parks every year, which suggests that zoos are very popular places. We all love to see animals that are not part of our daily landscape. We can watch the big apes or the giraffes or the antelopes for hours and keep coming back for more.

But modern, professionally run zoos, wildlife parks, and aquariums have more to do with educating people to the need for wildlife conservation than with entertainment. Much of the natural habitat of exotic animals is being destroyed, and in the process, entire species have become threatened, endangered, or extinct. Sometimes the zoo is the only place where an exotic species still exists.

And that is what a zoo is all about—maintaining animals for conservation. Zoos may house mammals, birds, reptiles, fish, and amphibians. Because of the variety of animals and their many needs, zoos provide abundant opportunities for employment.

Working in a Zoo or Wildlife Park

Although the animals in a zoo or wildlife park may be exotic, the actual work is not always glamorous. You need to be committed to conserving animal species through caring for individual animals to be an effective zoo worker. This kind of commitment requires long days of work, sometimes seven days a week, because the animals need round-the-clock care. And what are the rewards? Seeing well-cared-for animals who might otherwise not exist is often reward enough.

Because there are so few professionally operated zoos in North America, the competition for jobs is intense. The jobs and the duties involved are wide-ranging enough that you can probably find one that matches your skills and interest.

Education Requirements

Those who work directly with animals need a college degree, preferably in biology or zoology. Managers often need an advanced degree in animal sciences or business. In addition, you may have to take a written or oral examination to qualify for any zoo job in animal husbandry or administration.

Zookeeper

Zookeepers are the people who actually care for the animals on a day-to-day basis. The head zookeeper usually manages a specific department and is responsible for the staff of that department. Some zookeepers specialize in one particular type of animal, such as apes or the newborn and very young.

But the basic duty of the zookeeper is the daily care and maintenance of the animals. This means cleaning their living quarters and feeding them proper diets. Because zoos house exotic animals, much can be learned about them by carefully observing their habits, behavior, and preferences. Behavioral changes, however slight, may mean that something is wrong with the animal. The zookeeper is the one who may spot that change first.

Zookeepers need good communication skills. Because they are the people who work most closely with the animals and often know the most about them, they are called upon to explain the animals' routines, diets, and habits to visitors. Educating the public to the importance of conserving animal species is one of the primary responsibilities of the zoo, and the public relies on the zookeeper to be a general authority on animals.

Long Hours, Strenuous Work. Many zoo animals are very large, and their health care and feeding entails hard, strenuous labor, often for relatively low wages. The zookeeper has to be an educated professional on whom the animals can rely for their well-being and maintenance. Because of the possibility of sustaining injury inflicted by animals, the job can be seen as hazardous. As with anyone who takes care of animals, you may have to work occasional evenings, weekends, and holidays, because the animals' needs cannot be shut off at 5 P.M.

Even with these so-called disadvantages, zookeeping jobs are difficult to get. The small number of professionally operated zoos in the country and the large number of people applying for the available positions make for a stiff job market. The rewards of zookeeping are compelling enough—maintaining quality care for wild animals, including endangered species—that many people want to do this work. You may also advance to senior keeper and head keeper.

Becoming a Zookeeper. If you want to become a zookeeper, you need at least a high school diploma. Many zoos, however, now prefer applicants with college degrees, especially in biology, animal behavior, conservation biology, wildlife management, or zoology. Having biology in your high school curriculum will be helpful for any animal work but especially so for zookeeping. Any additional courses in animal science would put you ahead of the competition when it comes to applying for the job. You will probably experience a six-month on-the-job training period with your first position.

If you think you might like to work in a zoo, consider performing volunteer work during your summer break from school or on weekends, if you are presently employed. The more contact you have with animals and the people who work with animals, the better you will know whether this is a good career choice for you. And there is usually room for reliable, committed, and dedicated volunteer workers at most zoos.

Professional Organizations. In addition to your education and training, membership in a professional organization is strongly recommended in order to keep up with new ideas, meet other professional people, and share ideas. The American Association of Zoo Keepers promotes quality animal care and a professional attitude among zookeepers in the United States and Canada. The association provides members with conferences and individual chapters with specific activities. It also makes networking possible for members to exchange their experiences in animal care and treatment and other zoo-related matters.

The American Zoo and Aquarium Association can provide a list of potential employers. The American Association of Zoo Veterinarians is a professional group that focuses on those who are involved in captive-animal medicine. The American Association of Zoological Parks and Aquariums is the umbrella group for employees of zoos, aquariums, wildlife parks, and oceanariums.

Professional association members find the regularly scheduled meetings and conferences to be a highlight of their educational experiences and professional growth. Here members gather, both formally and informally, to discuss and debate specific topics. You will find that no matter how big or small your zoo may be, similar problems and challenges exist everywhere. Through exchanging information with other professionals, you can often discover solutions.

More Job Opportunities

Zoos require many different people and talents to operate smoothly. Most zoos have people working in the following positions: director, assistant director, curator, scientist, zookeeper, zoologist, gardener, public relations specialist, and clerical worker. Veterinarians, veterinary technicians, personnel specialists, operations managers, and business managers are also often needed. Many of these jobs are strictly administrative or are performed within the confines of the office. Others deal directly with the animals.

Many zoos also publish their own magazines and generate informational brochures, packets, and pamphlets, usually through their education or public-relations departments. Writers, editors, artists, and illustrators are needed to put these together. Guidebooks, maps, and information about specific animals have to be available for visitors. Zoos with gift shops need people with retail experience.

Zoo Director. The director of the zoo functions as the chief operating officer responsible for implementing policy and procedures for daily operations, in addition to mapping out any future growth and development needs. The director also serves as spokesperson for the institution. Often the director has an assistant director to help carry out these responsibilities.

Curator. The general curator is responsible for the whole animal collection. There also may be several other curators responsible for specific departments within the zoo. These positions may include curator of mammals, or birds, or fish; curator of exhibits; curator of education; or curator of research. As curator of mammals, for instance, you would be in charge of just that collection and would supervise all staff who work with mammals.

As the curator of exhibits, you would be responsible for the creation of permanent and special exhibitions. One of the most important functions of any zoo is to educate the public, and those programs are the responsibility of the curator of education. The curator of research manages all research programs and works closely with local colleges and universities.

Veterinarians, Veterinary Technicians, and Zoologists. Veterinarians and veterinary technicians are also employed at zoos. The veterinarian is responsible for the general health care of the whole animal population. Veterinarians keep detailed medical records of the animals in their care. Veterinary technicians assist the veterinarians in these responsibilities.

Zoologists oversee the future development of the animal collection. If any permits or licenses are needed to own certain animals, the zoologist obtains them.

Other Support Positions. All zoos need people who supervise and maintain the building and all its physical equipment. These are the operations managers, who usually have a staff of skilled workers under their supervision. Gardeners or horticulturists are responsible for the grounds, especially the animal habitats.

Most zoos have a public relations department that strives to get the good word out to the public about the institution and its purpose. Business managers, necessary for most of today's zoos, are in charge of finances. They pay all the bills, buy necessary equipment, issue paychecks to employees, and make investments. Human resource departments advertise to fill available positions and screen, interview, and evaluate applicants. A registrar may be employed to keep records on all the animals. Each of these departments also has a staff of clerical workers who are necessary for the smooth functioning of the zoo.

Employment Outlook

All in all, zookeepers and zoo support staff can find many rewards in their work, from preserving endangered species and maintaining a quality life for the animals to educating the public about conservation and maintaining the grounds and gardens. Observing the behavior, habits, and social patterns of an exotic animal and knowing that you are significantly helping to maintain the life of one of the few remaining members of that species often more than makes up for the long hours and strenuous work.

The future looks bright for those who choose a career in zoos and wildlife parks. If you are well prepared educationally and have some experience with animals, are willing to continue your professional growth and development, are reliable and cooperative, and above all, have compassion for animals, you have made an exciting career choice and should find a great deal of career satisfaction.

Working in an Aquarium

Like zoos, aquariums need both scientifically trained professionals to deal directly with animals and a large support staff to back up their efforts. Aquariums typically have an administrative and clerical staff, educational and research departments, operations managers, veterinarians and veterinary technicians, aquarists (aquarium keepers), and aquatic biologists.

Administrative and Support Positions

The top administrative person is the director, who has overall responsibility for the smooth functioning of the facility. An assistant director may also be on the staff. Various curators, personnel specialists, public-relations specialists, and clerical personnel are needed to staff the offices of an aquarium. A business manager and staff would round out the administrative end of the facility, and a librarian may also be employed at some aquariums. Researchers may use an aquarium's library for specialized studies of such topics as predator-prey relationships or population dynamics.

Operations managers and various technical workers, in addition to veterinarians and veterinary technicians who work alongside the aquarists and aquatic biologists, actually perform the daily tasks of maintaining the various species of marine life.

Education Requirements

Anyone working in the field of animal husbandry should have a college degree, either in biology or zoology, chemistry or physics.

A college degree is becoming more and more important for career advancement.

Some larger aquariums offer classes to elementary and high school students. It is not unusual for a large aquarium to have one hundred thousand schoolchildren visit the facility each year for educational programs and to see the realistic habitat exhibits. Some aquariums may even sponsor biology field trips for college or high school students to exotic marine locations such as the Bahamas. Participants go on snorkeling expeditions to identify and collect specimens to bring back to the aquarium. Sometimes special-interest groups, such as the Sierra Club or the Audubon Society, offer ecology camps, field days, and lectures for those who are thinking about getting into aquarium or zoological work.

If you are still in high school, you should take your general education curriculum very seriously, putting an emphasis on science, mathematics, and English. If you are still in college, it's a good idea to start your serious scientific course work before your junior year, then be ready to specialize by the time you are applying to graduate school. When you select a college or graduate school, be sure to talk to a career counselor or aquarist for the best advice on curriculum or requirements.

Becoming an Aquarist

Although it is preferable to have a college degree in order to become an aquarist, it may be possible under certain circumstances to work your way up through the ranks. If you are currently employed in another field, but think you might like to work in an aquarium, you can always begin by working as a volunteer, just to get a feel for the job. Volunteers can help out in a variety of ways, from feeding the fish and aquatic mammals to teaching basic skills to high school students. The more jobs you tackle as a volunteer, the more information you will have to make your career choice. As a college student, you might want to serve as an intern and gain valuable experience while earning college credit.

Another way to enter aquarium work is by way of a hobby. Anybody who owns a tank full of tropical fish will undoubtedly know about the care and feeding of their fish and something about filtration, diet, and breeding. Some may even work in pet shops specializing in fish. From there, it's a relatively easy transition to move from the small tanks of the shop to the huge tanks of the aquarium.

People who are currently working as aquarists can continue formal education by taking night courses to get an undergraduate or graduate degree. Many aquariums offer at least partial tuition reimbursement for these courses. Aquarists also continue to learn on the job and by reading trade journals and new books in the field. Membership in professional organizations and attendance at workshops and seminars also is part of ongoing education.

Employment Outlook
The aquarium, just like the zoo, is now primarily an educational and research facility with a need for highly skilled professionals at every level. Aquariums, like zoos, exist to conserve all manner of aquatic life, to maintain their health and well-being, and to educate the public to their needs. The American Association of Zoological Parks and Aquariums is the largest professional organization that sets the standards for those who work in aquariums and oceanariums. Through its work, the status of these workers has been consistently upgraded.

Aquarium work is often strenuous, and the hours may be long. Reliability, dedication, good physical health and strength, and love and compassion for the creatures in your care are the most important qualities of an aquarium worker.

Salaries awarded by both zoos and aquariums are probably not going to make you rich, but many offer health and retirement benefits as incentives. Basic annual salaries are generally higher in larger cities or larger facilities, which would also most likely provide greater room for advancement.

An Aquarium Curator

Allen Feldman, an assistant curator of fish, worked as an aquarist and aquatic biologist. He has a master's degree in aquatic biology.

Although Allen always thought he wanted to major in biology, he did not head straight for his goal. In college, he studied without focus for two years, not really getting a good science background. But he did become proficient in English, including writing, which he recommends for any aspiring aquatic biologist or administrator because writing reports and protocols is part of the job.

In his last two years as an undergraduate, Allen finally took mathematics, physics, biology, and chemistry. After college, he spent two and a half years in an immunology laboratory. But that kind of work did not satisfy him, so he took a job with the U.S. Department of Agriculture performing qualitative and quantitative analyses on condiments. By that time, he really knew that he wanted to work with animals in some capacity.

He had also, over the years, become an animal hobbyist, keeping fish tanks at home and watching birds on weekends. He started sending his resume to various zoos and aquariums and got back the usual number of rejections—except from the Shedd Aquarium. His degree, as well as his previous laboratory work, helped him get his first job at an aquarium. He worked for a year and a half as an aquarist before being promoted to aquatic biologist.

As an aquatic biologist, he had more authority and was in a better position to become an assistant curator—which is exactly what happened. But before he got the promotion, he coordinated major projects, such as moving fish from tank to tank as they grew and needed more space. He was also responsible for overseeing the total needs of the fish in his care. This work entailed diagnostic work and bacterial study, proper use of antibiotics for diseased animals, estimating compatibility of different fish, and establishing quarantine procedures. Because the tank is where the fish carry on all their activities, from eating to eliminating waste, they are prone to disease both from toxins and from stress.

Allen was also responsible for providing basic nutritional and dietary requirements to every species, for husbandry, and for chemical analysis of the water. Because little was known about the nutritional requirements of some of the more exotic fish, it sometimes became necessary to perform research in this area. Allen was also concerned with any problems with the tanks, filtration system, and pumps.

In many aquariums, both managerial and technical skills are necessary at this level, for even though you are supervising other aquarists, you are also probably spending about 90 percent of your time directly with the fish. Only 10 percent of your time may actually involve coordinating and scheduling programs and dealing with personnel problems.

One of the major problems aquarists have with their jobs is that they feel they are not regarded with the same respect that other scientists enjoy. Allen and others contend that aquarists are not just tank cleaners but, rather, animal behaviorists and conservationists. In the past, there was less respect for aquatic species, too. Earlier in this century, according to Allen, many aquariums collected randomly and indiscriminately.

In the last few decades, the aquarist and aquatic biologist have become more and more professional in their work as collectors and educators. Today's aquarists collect only those animals that are needed to complete their facilities' collections or to save an endangered species. They can then breed that species in captivity in order to preserve future generations.

Although the pay for aquarium workers is not high and the workers do not always get the respect they deserve, Allen thinks that there are some distinct advantages to this career. Most aquarists and aquatic biologists really love what they do. They work cooperatively as members of a highly motivated and dedicated team and get real job satisfaction from their work. In a way, they get to be biology students forever because they never stop learning from their aquatic charges.

Aquarists and aquatic biologists do get to travel throughout the country for meetings and lectures where they exchange ideas and information with others. Allen has also been on some scuba-diving and collecting trips to the Bahamas and Puerto Rico and on a troubleshooting mission to the Dominican Republic.

Allen thinks it is an advantage to work for an employer that has no dress code except shorts and jeans and gym shoes. Aquariums also often have generous vacation and holiday schedules and free medical insurance. And although you may not become a millionaire as an aquarium employee, Allen thinks that you are really rich when you are doing what you love to do. He loves his work, enjoys going to work each day, and hopes to continue in his career for a long time to come.

He also believes that now is a very good time for people to seek work in aquariums because so many new aquariums are opening, professional organizations are upgrading the status of aquarists and aquatic biologists, and new knowledge and information is constantly being brought forth to make the work even more challenging.

Working as an Ornithologist

Ornithology, the scientific study of birds, offers many careers that cover a variety of aspects of bird life, such as behavior, ecology, anatomy and physiology, veterinary science, wildlife management, and conservation. As with other animal-related fields, career possibilities are offered in management, fieldwork, teaching, and research. It is a highly competitive field, so education and training will be your key into a career in ornithology.

Education Requirements

At the very least, you will need a bachelor's degree to become an ornithologist; to attain the top positions in the field, a doctorate is required. Note that course work and emphases vary between schools. Before you choose which school to attend or which courses to take, confer with a professor or career counselor to ensure that your academic choices are heading you in the right direction.

In college, you should study biology, zoology, mathematics, physical sciences, and biochemistry. You should develop your communications skills, obtaining a knowledge of a foreign language as well as a mastery of spoken and written English. Research work, publications, and recommendations from your instructors will help you get accepted at a top-quality graduate school.

Your choice of graduate schools is crucial to the development of your career. It is in graduate school that you will begin to specialize in a specific aspect of ornithology or animal science. You will branch out into independent research and perhaps assist in teaching laboratory courses.

An advanced degree in zoology from an institution well known as a center of ornithology, ecology, or wildlife management will put you ahead of the competition when looking for a job. You also want to match your school to your particular interests, such as systematics (the science of classification of living organisms) or biology. Sometimes the best way to find out about a school, besides reading the catalog and talking to counselors, is to actually visit the school and talk to faculty and students. Graduate work may last four to five years for a doctorate, and most counselors advise that you try to publish articles in scientific journals during that time.

A comprehensive listing of U.S. and Canadian colleges and graduate schools can be found in volume one of *The College Blue Book*, usually available in the public library. This is a good starting point for your research into the correct choice of school.

As with most jobs that offer direct work with animals, you should gain practical experience with birds before you decide to become an ornithologist. Many budding ornithologists start out as bird-watchers. You may want to join a local bird-watching club, where you can meet other people with the same interests. Or you may decide to work as a volunteer at a university, national park, wildlife refuge, bird sanctuary, zoo, or museum. As a volunteer, you might be asked to band particular species in the field, gather data, or do research. Any kind of hands-on training you can obtain, in combination with your education, will put you in a very good position for employment.

Job Opportunities for Ornithologists

Many ornithologists serve as teachers at educational institutions, while others work for state or federal agencies. Museums and research organizations also employ professional ornithologists. Some ornithologists work as administrators, while others combine teaching and research skills.

Because the competition for ornithological jobs is keen, you might consider a related field where jobs are more plentiful. Such fields would include toxicology, wildlife management, paleontology, physiology, and endocrinology. The following sections describe some of the employment options for ornithologists and related specialists.

Teaching. Teaching at a college or university is a career choice of many people working in North America in some aspect of ornithology. At larger universities, research may be a large part of your work. The career track at a university usually begins with the title of instructor or assistant professor, leading to associate professor and to full professor. Your base pay may be supplemented through research grants or by lecturing or consulting professionally in the field.

In addition to having your doctorate in zoology, biology, or ornithology, you must have highly developed communications skills and a solid educational background. You will be interviewed extensively and may have to give seminars on your research before being hired as an entry-level instructor.

Museums and Zoos. If you choose museum work, you may specialize in research, become a curator, or engage in fieldwork all over the world. Or you may work in the aviary or education department or help put together exhibits and publications. Curators are in charge of the collections, but there are only a few positions as ornithological curator available in this country.

With a master's degree, you may work in the ornithology department of a museum as a collection manager, technician, or preparator. Mastery of the computer is becoming increasingly important for the creation of databases on museum collections.

Zoos also employ ornithologists as curators and keepers, but these positions are rare. Curators at zoos usually need just a bachelor's degree and some previous experience with captive animals.

Federal and State Agencies. Federal and state agencies also employ ornithologists, especially those with some background in ecology. Jobs are available through the U.S. Fish and Wildlife Service, the National Park Service, and the National Forest Service. Most of the jobs offered by the federal government involve wildlife management, conservation, and the preservation of endangered species. State fish and game agencies have recently been developing studies on threatened and endangered species, so professionally trained field ornithologists will be needed for these positions.

The Private Sector. Private-sector organizations also employ ornithologists as administrators, policy makers, and researchers, often to run sanctuaries. These organizations include the National Audubon Society, the Nature Conservancy, and the National Wildlife Federation, which publishes the *Conservation Directory*. This directory is a fund of knowledge for private conservation organizations. Ornithologist positions in private companies are also starting to open up. These jobs may include conducting natural history tours or setting up conservation and environmental policies for the company.

In Canada. If you choose to work as an ornithologist in Canada, your chances for employment are even slimmer than they are in the United States. A limited number of teaching jobs are available at universities. Provincial wildlife agencies hire some wildlife managers, but museum jobs are few. Because Canada is a bilingual country, knowledge of both French and English is helpful for any employment. Otherwise, the qualifications are more or less equivalent to those for similar positions in the United States.

Seasonal work can be found with the Canadian Wildlife Service, but the number of permanent positions is limited. Private companies also hire few ornithologists, but administrative and fundraising positions are available in environmental consulting firms and similar organizations.

Whichever career path you choose, you must prepare carefully in order to be ready to compete for the limited number of jobs available in education, research, museums, and fieldwork, both in the United States and in Canada. If you are fully qualified, however, and have previous experience with birds, your chances for permanent employment with a secure future are good.

For More Information

Publications

Camenson, Blythe. *Opportunities in Zoos and Aquariums.* McGraw-Hill, 1997.

Catchpole, C. K., and P. J. B. Slater. *Bird Song: Biological Themes and Variations.* Cambridge University Press, 2003.

Line, Les, and Franklin Russell, eds. *National Audubon Society Book of Wild Birds.* Wings Books, 1997.

National Audubon Society Field Guide to Tropical Marine Fishes. Alfred A. Knopf Inc., 1997.

Robinson, Phillip T. *Life at the Zoo: Behind the Scenes with the Animal Doctors.* Columbia University Press, 2004.

Associations

American Association of Zoo Keepers (AAZK)
3601 Southwest Twenty-Ninth Street, Suite 133
Topeka, KS 66614
www.aazk.org

American Association of Zoo Veterinarians
581705 White Oak Road
Yulee, FL 32097
www.aazv.org

American Ornithologists' Union
1313 Dolley Madison Boulevard, Suite 402
McLean, VA 22101
www.aou.org

Association of American Zoos and Aquariums (AZA)
8403 Colesville Road, Suite 710
Silver Spring, MD 20910
www.aza.org

National Audubon Society
700 Broadway
New York, NY 10003
www.audubon.org

World Association of Zoos and Aquariums (WAZA)
PO Box 23
CH-3097 Libefeld-Bern
Switzerland
www.waza.org

CHAPTER EIGHT

Preserving and Conserving Wildlife

B oth the federal government and individual states administer agencies that deal with wildlife preservation and the conservation of natural resources. Chief among the federal employers in this area is the Department of the Interior, which includes the National Park Service and the U.S. Fish and Wildlife Service. More limited in their job offerings are the Department of Agriculture, which includes the National Forest Service, and the Department of Commerce. Other federal agencies, such as the Bureau of Land Management, the Bureau of Indian Affairs, and some military bases, have limited employment opportunities for those interested in animal work.

Each state has a fish and wildlife agency, and there are a growing number of private wildlife protective organizations that target a particular species for preservation and protection. Somewhere among all these choices, you may find a lifetime career.

The Department of the Interior

The Department of the Interior, with headquarters in Washington, D.C., has seven regional offices, as well as field units, installations, and a fleet of law enforcement agents throughout the country. It manages more than five hundred million acres of land and water, with more than five hundred wildlife refuges protecting nearly two thousand endangered or threatened species. The department is responsible for improving habitat for migratory birds, marine mammals, and sport fisheries.

The department has developed ecological principles and scientific knowledge of wildlife that it shares with state agencies, and it tries to involve the American public in understanding and wisely using our natural resources. Resource management includes improving and maintaining proper habitats for fish and wildlife. The department also issues environmental impact reviews based on impact assessments.

Specific programs that the Department of the Interior administers include:

- Coordination with foreign governments
- Federal endangered and threatened species list
- Foreign importation enforcement
- Great Lakes fisheries
- Invasive species control
- Law enforcement in national parks, refuges, and other public lands
- Migratory bird protection
- Educational and recreational programs, such as self-guided nature trails and interpretive centers
- Visitor centers
- Wildlife recovery plans
- Wildlife refuge management

Regional offices are in Albuquerque, New Mexico; Anchorage, Alaska; Atlanta, Georgia; Hadley, Massachusetts; Portland, Oregon; Minneapolis–St. Paul, Minnesota; and Denver, Colorado.

Because it is responsible for almost all public lands and natural resources in the country, it is also the nation's largest federal conservation agency. In its purview are the National Park Service and the U.S. Fish and Wildlife Service (USFWS). Most jobs having to do with wildlife are found in the USFWS, with fewer at the

National Park Service. The U.S. Fish and Wildlife Service mission is to "conserve, manage, protect, and enhance fish, wildlife, plants, and their habitats for the continuing benefit of all Americans."

The U.S. Office of Personnel Management (OPM) maintains a register where you may be listed once you establish your eligibility for available positions. It administers federal job information and testing offices throughout the country where all appropriate application forms are available.

A great deal of information is available online at the following websites:

- Department of the Interior: www.doi.gov
- U.S. Fish and Wildlife Service: www.fws.gov
- USFWS Division of Habitat Conservation: www.habitat.fws.gov
- Office of Personnel Management (OPM): www.usajobs.opm.gov

At the OPM website, you can search for jobs in specific regions or by department. You will find general information and application forms, and you can create resumes custom designed to apply for federal jobs, which can then be printed for faxing to employers and saved for future editing.

The three-step process for applying for a position with the federal government is as follows:

1. Use the job-search feature to find job openings for which you might qualify.
2. Obtain a vacancy announcement, which includes the closing date for the job, testing and educational requirements, and salary. These can be found online at www.usajobs.com. You can also find employment information fact sheets, application forms, and resume development tools on the website.

3. Follow the instructions for applying with an OF-612 form and a resume that includes current employment, education, work experience, and other qualifications for the job. You can transmit completed forms electronically or use the automated telephone system, which is listed in the federal government pages of your local telephone book. Or visit one of the seventeen OPM locations for applications and information.

Requirements and Qualifications for Employment

All federal government employees are hired at a certain General Schedule (GS) level. These standards are published by the OPM in *The Qualifications Standards Handbook for General Schedule Positions*. This handbook, available at local libraries, lists general policies and instructions, including educational requirements; individual occupational requirements; knowledge, skills, and abilities required; specialized experience preferred; and the normal line of promotion. The handbook also explains about veteran's preferences and waivers of requirements and contains an explanation of the qualifying educational requirements for various GS levels. For example, a GS-5 applicant should have a bachelor's degree or four academic years beyond high school leading to a bachelor's degree. A GS-7 applicant should have a bachelor's degree with superior academic achievement or one academic year of graduate school or law school, and a GS-9 position requires a master's degree or the equivalent.

The USFWS will accept your application if you are within nine months of completing your requirements, but you must prove that you have completed the required course work before you can actually be hired. You will be eligible at one level for one year from the time of hire, at which time you must submit a written request to the examining officer. With additional education or experience, you may become eligible to apply for a higher grade. The higher the GS level you qualify for, the higher your salary.

By law, all departments of the federal government are equal-opportunity employers, which means that your religion, race, color, national origin, sex, age, or disability will not be considered as a term of employment.

The federal government leaves very little to the imagination for those who wish to apply for a job. So don't expect loopholes, exceptions, or exclusions if you are considering a career as a civil servant. The requirements are quite clearly spelled out, and competition for jobs is fierce. You must learn the many rules of eligibility and comply with them if you hope to get a federal job. Correspondence courses in conservation, for example, are generally not acceptable to the USFWS, and most applicants must pass a written test to be added to the jobs register. Contact the nearest OPM job information center to learn more about examinations. Often many more candidates apply for a job than there are jobs available. When this happens, the register is suspended and no new applications are accepted by the OPM.

Working for the U.S. Fish and Wildlife Service

Once you have fulfilled all the employment requirements and have been hired, what kind of job might you expect to perform? The USFWS offers jobs that are primarily concerned with wildlife management. Generally, the jobs involve managing and studying various aspects of fish and wildlife, such as habitat, populations, ecology, and health and mortality statistics. Here are a few job descriptions with the USFWS for animal lovers.

Wildlife and Research Biologist. Wildlife biologists at the USFWS plan wildlife programs, apply research results to sound wildlife management, manipulate populations, restore damaged habitats, and prevent wildlife diseases.

The job of research biologist consists largely of studying wildlife populations as well as relationships between plants and animals. Research biologists also investigate the physiology of wildlife and their nutritional needs. They take census counts and study predator-prey relationships.

If you want to be a wildlife biologist, you need a college degree in biological science with course work that includes nine hours in mammalogy, ornithology, animal ecology, and wildlife management. You should also have twelve hours of general zoology, comparative anatomy, physiology, ecology, entomology, and wildlife biology.

Fishery Biologist. Like wildlife biologists, fishery biologists are involved in a range of conservation activities. They restore aquatic habitat, preserve endangered species, monitor fish populations, and study and apply the best methods for rearing fish and stocking fisheries.

To qualify as a fishery biologist, you need a college degree in biological science with six semester hours in aquatic subjects, such as limnology, fishery biology, aquatic botany, aquatic fauna, oceanography, fish culture, or related courses. You should have at least twelve semester hours in subjects such as general zoology, vertebrate zoology, comparative anatomy, physiology, cellular biology, and genetics.

Refuge Manager. Managers of wildlife refuges try to protect all species of wildlife and fish, whether they are indigenous or migratory. They also enforce hunting and fishing regulations as they apply to the refuges and other public lands.

To qualify as a refuge manager, you need a college degree in biology, wildlife management, or an appropriate field of biology that includes at least nine semester hours in general zoology, six hours in courses such as mammalogy, ornithology, animal ecology, or wildlife management, and nine semester hours in botany. Or you could have a combination of education and experience.

Outdoor Recreation Planner or Ranger. Outdoor recreation planners and rangers educate the community about conservation issues and coordinate wildlife-related recreational activities, such as tours, nature walks, and educational events. They may also organize special hunting or fishing programs.

In order to qualify for the position, you must have knowledge of natural resources and conservation issues. You must be able to integrate public uses of wildlife refuges and fish hatcheries with conservation needs. Your communications skills should be highly developed because you are responsible for various interpretative and educational programs.

For most positions, you need at least a bachelor's degree in outdoor recreation planning, park administration, natural resource management, landscape architecture, or biology. Additionally, you must have experience in a professional, managerial, or technical capacity in outdoor recreation planning, conservation, or a related field. Specific positions may require additional skills in graphic arts, interpretative display, or environmental programming.

Special Wildlife Agent. There are a limited number of positions available for special wildlife agents, whose job it is to enforce wildlife laws and regulations. Special agents conduct investigations and prepare cases for court. They are also involved in public education.

To qualify above entry level, you must have experience in both enforcement and investigation regarding all fish and wildlife rules or graduate study in law enforcement, police management, criminal justice, or biology.

Other Positions. Wildlife inspectors are stationed at major international airports, ocean ports, and border crossings to guard against illegal trade in wildlife. Refuge officers are law enforcement officers who prevent poaching on national wildlife refuges. Engineers plan and design the facilities needed on wildlife refuges. External affairs specialists work with state agencies, Native American tribes, Congress, and the news media to provide information about USFWS activities.

Like any large bureaucracy, the USFWS needs administrative, clerical, and creative people to help it function smoothly. Among these are clerks and secretaries, personnel and public relations specialists, budget analysts and accountants, writers, editors, and economists. Biological technicians, fishery and wildlife technicians, maintenance people, and craftspeople are also utilized.

Gaining Experience as a Volunteer

The USFWS has a wide variety of opportunities for volunteers. If you want to determine whether you are suited to wildlife or fishery work, you could serve as a volunteer helping with the census of wildlife populations. This work entails banding, trapping, and surveying. Or you could become involved in the care and feeding of animals.

If you like to work with people, you may want to work with visitor services. Specialists in computer programming, audiovisual work, or photography are also needed. Each field station has different needs, so you should contact the one nearest you to find out where you could be of help.

Volunteers come in all shapes, sizes, and ages. They include senior citizens and Boy Scout troops. You can volunteer with no particular skills and receive the necessary training when you are accepted. Hours are flexible and sometimes are arranged on a project basis. You will only work the hours that you agree to in advance. You may work as an individual volunteer or as a member of an organized group, such as a 4-H club. As a volunteer, you will receive an agreement that defines your duties and the number of hours you have agreed on to fulfill them. The agreement can be revised at any time, but it serves as an official record of your service and could be used to enhance your resume. This will be especially helpful should you decide to make a career of conservation. You can also receive an evaluation of your performance, if you want.

Even though as a volunteer you are not considered a federal employee, you are entitled to some benefits. They include compensation if you are injured in the line of duty. If you were sued for damage to property or personal injury while serving as a volunteer, the federal government would defend you. Also, certain expenses incurred during your volunteer service with the USFWS would be tax deductible. But volunteer service does not count as civil service time.

Wildlife refuges, fish hatcheries, and research stations in all states need volunteers, but the needs in each continually change. Volunteering for the USFWS is an excellent first step in helping you determine whether you want to work in this area of wildlife conservation.

Working for the National Park Service

The Department of the Interior employs a more limited number of people to work with animals in the National Park Service. The service maintains more than 375 units, including national parks and monuments, scenic parkways, preserves, trails, river ways, seashores, lakeshores, and recreation areas. The six regional centers are located in Anchorage, Alaska; Denver, Colorado; Omaha, Nebraska; Washington, D.C.; Philadelphia, Pennsylvania; and San Francisco, California.

The service is charged with the mission of developing and implementing park management plans and administering the state portion of the Land and Water Conservation Fund. It is also responsible for planning and giving technical assistance for the National Wild and Scenic Rivers System, the National Trails System, and other natural-area programs.

The National Park Service employs thousands of full-time personnel, and at peak season during the summer, that number swells with seasonal, temporary, and part-time employees. As with the U.S. Fish and Wildlife Service, all positions are filled through the Office of Personnel Management.

Because many park jobs are located away from cities, potential employees must be able to relocate in order to be employed. All positions are very competitive, so you must be highly qualified to be considered for employment. The National Park Service, like all federal agencies, is an equal opportunity employer. The service employs interpreters, resource managers, and research scientists for its parks, historic sites, and recreation areas. Some of the larger parks have research centers, and the service also administers resource studies units at several universities.

Within the National Park Service, there are limited employment opportunities for wildlife and fish biologists and ornithologists; there are a few more for research biologists. Usually these positions are above the GS-5 and GS-7 level and require advanced degrees or work experience in specialized fields.

Working for a State Conservation Agency

If you decide that working for the federal government is not for you, you may want to consider working for a state conservation agency. All fifty states have such agencies, and most do similar work. Their names may vary somewhat, but they are usually called the Department of Fish, Wildlife, and Parks; the Department of Natural Resources; or the Fish and Game Commission. Most are headquartered in the state capital. Each state has a website that will direct you to the specific agency.

Although job titles and salaries vary from state to state, the following information is somewhat typical for all states. For example, the state agency's primary responsibility is the preservation of fish, plant, and wildlife resources. State agencies are similar to their federal counterparts in that they are equal-opportunity employers, their employees are civil servants, and they usually have specific qualifications and application procedures for the jobs.

Most states have employment websites that provide all the qualifications, salary ranges, job titles and descriptions, educational and training requirements, locations of testing facilities, physical requirements, and any other pertinent information you may need to make your career decisions.

Education Requirements

Some state agencies recommend that you start thinking about a conservation career by the time you get to high school. One indication that you might be cut out for this work would be your choice of hobbies and leisure activities. If they include bird-watching, fishing, nature photography, or similar activities having to do with nature and animals, you might enjoy working with fish and wildlife conservation.

If you're in high school now, you should take biology, physics, chemistry, and mathematics. Since you will also have to be able to interpret complex and technical information for laypeople, a mastery of spoken and written English is essential. Some knowledge of geography and the earth sciences is also helpful.

Because most careers in the natural resource sciences require at least a bachelor's degree, you should carefully consider which college or university you will attend. It is a good idea to talk with your counselor or with members of the faculty at the schools you are considering. Consulting the professional organization affiliated with your specialty is also helpful. Two such organizations are the American Fisheries Society and the Wildlife Conservation Society.

High school and college are good times to get involved in extracurricular activities, such as debating or writing for the school newspaper. These will help prepare you for public speaking and report writing.

In your undergraduate years, you should concentrate on expanding your knowledge in a variety of areas, such as humanities, English composition, literature, mathematics, history, geography, foreign language, and science, including biology, chemistry, zoology, physics, and computer science. When you have chosen your major, such as zoology, you should take some of the more specialized courses within that discipline, such as invertebrate zoology, physiology, or systematics.

If you want to move up the career ladder, you should seriously consider getting a master's or doctoral degree. You would then specialize in some aspect of your conservation career choice. The positions that usually require master's degrees and beyond include teaching, research, management, and administration. If you become a teacher, state conservation agencies may call on you as a consultant in your specialized field.

Physical Qualifications

In addition to your education and training, some states may have rather strict physical standards as qualifications of employment. Prospective employees may be screened for physical conditions that could serve as disqualifiers in some states: alcoholism, allergies, bronchitis, diabetes, heart disease, hemophilia, hypertension, and psychotic disease.

Positions Available in State Conservation Agencies

The field of natural resources conservation and wildlife management needs highly trained professionals who have a broad educational background combined with very specific skills. Here are some typical job titles for positions within the state agencies:

- Fish and Game Biologist
- Fish and Game Warden
- Fish and Wildlife Assistant
- Fish and Wildlife Interpreter
- Fishery Biologist
- Fish Manager
- Game Protector
- Natural Resources Specialist
- Wildlife Agent
- Wildlife Biologist
- Wildlife Enforcement Officer
- Wildlife Information and Education Specialist
- Wildlife Interpreter
- Wildlife Manager

- Wildlife Officer
- Wildlife Research Biologist

Fish and Game Wardens

Fish and game wardens enforce the rules and regulations of the individual state's fish and game commission. This work usually entails patrolling specific areas and investigating results of environmental pollution and destruction of habitats. Wardens also coordinate their activities of collecting and reporting information with other departments. They are often called on to inspect commercial enterprises where fish and game are handled or sold.

Law enforcement on public lands also involves surveying fish and wildlife and teaching classes on hunter safety, trapping, or fishing. Field investigators can yield many arrests per year, especially for poaching or for water pollution violations that lead to the deaths of wild animals or fish. For this position, only two years of college are generally required, with an emphasis on the study of biology and law enforcement.

Fish and Wildlife Assistants

Fish and wildlife assistants may raise fish at fish hatcheries, release game birds, or maintain animal cages. They may take animal censuses or trap, tag, or mark fish or wildlife. For this position, you generally need only one year of college with some course work in biology, as well as some work experience at parks, forests, or fisheries.

Wildlife and Fishery Biologists

Wildlife biologists for the state may be involved in basic research, environmental protection studies, or various field activities, such as observing, tagging, and banding birds or wildlife or surveying animal foraging patterns. Wildlife biologists may also collect certain species, work in the laboratory, develop animal habitats, and meet with visitors.

Habitat loss for wild animals is becoming an increasingly common problem because of so much land development and environmental pollution. Preserving habitat in many cases preserves the species, so this work is extremely important for the total environment and is, therefore, a major part of the work of the wildlife biologist.

To qualify for the position of wildlife biologist with most state agencies, you need a bachelor of science degree in zoology, botany, wildlife management, or a related subject.

Most states employ aquatic biologists for their fish hatcheries. These employees are involved in research, fishery management, and data collection. They may also survey populations and capture and tag species for analysis in the laboratory. Land and water projects could alter aquatic life, and the aquatic biologist may be called on to evaluate the effects of such projects on the life of the fish. Sometimes they have to write reports on their findings. A bachelor's degree or equivalent is necessary for this position, with biology, fishery management, or marine biology as a major.

Wildlife Interpreters

A fish and wildlife interpreter plans, develops, and coordinates interpretative programs. In doing so, they must reduce sometimes highly technical information to a level that is understandable to the public. These employees are also called on to lecture to community groups, civic organizations, and schools. Sometimes they present slide shows or conduct tours to provide information about fishing, small animals, and other natural resources.

In addition to having a bachelor's degree in zoology, wildlife or fishery management, or botany, interpreters generally must successfully complete courses in natural resource interpretation or communications or equivalent course work.

Working Conditions and Benefits

Let's say that you have filled the requirements of a wildlife or fish biologist and have gotten a job with your state natural resources department. What are the benefits, and can you advance in your career? Although your commitment to improve the health and living conditions of animals may give you career satisfaction, you still need to pay rent and buy food. And, in most cases, you can make more money in the private sector than as a civil servant. So what motivates people to go into this kind of work?

Some people point to the progressive career tracks that many agencies offer as motivators. Promotions, for example, may come in the first two years in some states. You receive regular performance evaluations and career counseling if needed. Your evaluations can be valuable aids in letting you know how you can improve your work. You will probably have to go through a probation period of a few months before you are reviewed, but if your work is satisfactory, you will be in a good position for promotion.

In addition to career advancement possibilities, many states offer a generous benefits package, including health, life, dental, and disability insurance plans; paid sick days, holidays, and vacations; retirement plans; and credit unions.

Advancing to Management

Both areas of conservation—fish and wildlife—have career tracks that lead to management positions. An intermediate stage between biologist and regional manager may be referred to as senior biologist, biologist II, or wildlife or fishery manager.

A fish and wildlife manager works closely with administrative personnel and is more involved with planning programs and activities or working with other state agencies on matters of fish and wildlife policy. This level, then, has largely to do with strategy, policy making, planning, and coordination of projects that may have a statewide impact on wildlife. You would formulate research methods, submit reports, and evaluate and recommend projects.

You may also be called on to acquire more public land in order to develop more habitats, in which case you must set priorities and establish guidelines for the acquisition. This may involve appraisals, determining purchasing requirements, negotiations, and budget meetings. It also requires your knowledge of laws and regulations regarding land acquisition and use. Environmental impact studies may have to be generated at this stage of the process.

As reports come to your desk, you are responsible for analyzing and evaluating them. Therefore, you need to have wide-ranging knowledge—of ecology; plant, animal, and fish dynamics; feeding needs; behavioral patterns; and habitats—in order to implement recommendations based on the results of research.

Your communications skills come in handy at the managerial level because you may have to write technical reports for statewide distribution regarding your plans and programs. You may also write articles for trade journals or for popular consumption.

Any work done by state employees requires disclosure to the public. The reports you prepare may be for consumption not only by other scientists or state officials but also by the citizens of the state. You may be required to present these reports orally to groups of constituents, or you may speak at community or school events or scientific conferences. Or you may appear on radio or television shows for informational purposes.

A knowledge of your state's geography will help you plan programs that ensure an improved environment for all forms of life in the area. In some cases, you may have to interpret aerial photographs of land areas to determine how those areas might best be utilized. In many cases, you may also have to use computers to compile and analyze field data and store the information in a database.

You may also plan and organize large research projects. In the process, you will work out costs and budgeting considerations, allocate funds, oversee equipment purchases and repairs, and supervise researchers and other staff members.

As manager of a staff, you set policy, procedures, and priorities for your employees. If you use outside services, you have to review contracts and supervise and evaluate their work. You conduct staff meetings to get information on the progress of all projects under your supervision. You set deadlines and make assignments for those projects and ensure that the proper methods are employed in carrying them out. You see to it that your staff has the equipment, funds, and outside help they need.

In most states, you must have a master of science degree and knowledge of the ecology and geography of your region or state. Your work affects not only wildlife and fish; it may impact a wide range of elements within the community, including business, law enforcement, recreation, real estate, land development, and education.

As a fish manager, you may be additionally responsible for setting standards of regulation for the spawning and harvesting of fish, protecting fish populations, and taking part in committee work that oversees these regulations. You may even be involved in making state laws regarding use of fish by ensuring that legislators have the proper background material and that sound fish management principles are incorporated into any proposed statutes. In this aspect of the job, you would testify at public hearings, prepared with essential facts and data.

As you advance in your career from biologist to manager, you will probably be less and less involved in the day-to-day contact with animals. But you can be consoled by the fact that all your planning, strategizing, writing, reporting, testifying, coordinating, developing, and evaluating will serve to improve the environment of the fish and wildlife in your jurisdiction.

Remember that each state has different educational requirements, job titles and descriptions, salary ranges, and benefits. This overview is intended to give you a brief idea of the possibilities available to you as a member of a natural resources department. Be sure to contact the specific agency in your state for a more precise, specific, and thorough explanation of employment procedures.

Some states might recommend that you work on a seasonal or part-time basis as a volunteer before you make up your mind about working with wildlife and fish populations. All states are looking for enthusiastic, dependable, and reliable employees who are also thoroughly trained professionals. Above all, state fish and wildlife workers must be committed to the animals' welfare.

Working for Private-Sector Conservation Organizations

If you decide to work for wildlife in the private sector, there are many nonprofit organizations that work toward the conservation and preservation of threatened, endangered, or tortured animal species. These organizations operate independently of any state or federal agencies and are sometimes at odds with them on matters of basic policy. Some conflicts arise concerning land use that may destroy habitats for many animals; others may have to do with methods of killing aquatic life.

Some of these organizations are international in scope; others, domestic. Some strive for the preservation of whole ecological systems; others, for one particular species. Still others object to the use of certain traps or nets that may inadvertently kill another already threatened species. Some work toward the abolition of poaching or trade in a specific animal product.

People who work for governmental agencies must follow the policies of the particular administration in power at the time. Since private organizations are independent of governmental dictates as to philosophy and strategy, they are free to pursue their goals as they see them.

Positions Available in the Private Sector

Nonprofit organizations may not have employment eligibility requirements as strict as those of government agencies, but they do need fully qualified scientists and lawyers; personnel and public relations specialists; and administrative, clerical, and creative people.

The job titles may vary from organization to organization. Some may combine functions and responsibilities. Top positions may include the president or chief executive officer, who may have assistants or deputies. Generally, these organizations also employ a corporate counsel, marketing director, business officer, controller, and administrative director.

Chief executive officers oversee all staff and operations. Their deputies work in conjunction with these top administrators and often stand in for them when they are absent. Legal counsel serve as advisers to the staff and often coordinate outside legal help. The marketing directors supervise a staff that develops products and services, advertising, and promotions, in addition to performing market research. Business managers see to the daily financial and administrative needs of the organization, while the controller supervises the financial staff. Directors of administration are responsible for all operations within the office, such as maintaining space, equipment, and supplies.

Some nonprofit organizations also employ computer specialists, including managers and analysts, who design and write programs, analyze systems, and produce reports. Benefits and affirmative action plans, organizational policy, staff records, and recruiting are all handled by the personnel or human resources department. Directors of development supervise a staff of fundraisers and assist local chapters where needed. Developing a steady list of donors, foundations, and corporate contributors is crucial to nonprofit organizations because they are not supported by public funds, as are government agencies.

The public relations department prepares and distributes informational newsletters, magazines, pamphlets, brochures, and direct-mail pieces to the public that present the work of the organization. The activities of these specialists may also include appearances on radio and television shows and at special events or community meetings.

Private organizations depend on membership for support for their causes and for financial stability. The membership staff is responsible for developing services to promote new membership and keep existing members.

Research is also vital to these organizations, so there is usually a research group that compiles and analyzes statistics for management. They must also be able to translate the data into reports and recommendations.

There also may be a need for long-range program or planning directors, project directors, and field service representatives, as well as volunteer coordinators. The project director may work on carefully designed ad hoc projects that only last a certain time and have a specific purpose. Field service representatives work as liaisons between the national organization and the local chapters.

Critical for nonprofit organizations are the government relations director and public policy specialist. Government relations directors represent the organization's interests in its relationships with Congress and other government agencies. They may also be responsible for obtaining government contracts and grants for the organization. Public policy specialists gather and analyze legislative information and distribute it to the national headquarters or local affiliates. They may also be responsible for working with the government relations staff.

Positions within private-sector organizations, as in state agencies, may vary in title, specific responsibilities, and salary. You will want to contact the organizations individually if you are interested in working for them.

Many of these organizations employ fieldworkers who are in more direct contact with wildlife and wildlife habitat, including scientists, biologists, ecologists, and environmental specialists, depending on the specific purpose of the organization. These positions generally require a bachelor's degree; for managerial positions, such as refuge manager, a master's degree is required.

Private-Sector Organizations in Operation

Let's now take a look at some of these private organizations to give you an idea of the range of intent, purpose, and operation.

World Wildlife Fund. One of the older and better-known private-sector wildlife organizations is the World Wildlife Fund (WWF). Established in 1961, it claims a worldwide membership of 1.2 million people. Its mission is to protect biological resources and to preserve endangered and threatened wildlife and plants and their habitats. In other words, the fund deals with the preservation of all threatened wildlife—even though only the panda appears on its famous logo. Its activities are scientifically based to provide conservation models for ecological planning and policies. The fund assists any public or private conservation organizations that move these projects and services forward.

The WWF, then, is concerned with preserving not only species but whole ecological systems, such as tropical rain forests. These ancient forests, home for half of all wildlife species and many plants and trees from which lifesaving medicines are extracted, are threatened by commercial exploitation and environmental pollution. Grasslands, wetlands, and oceans are also being polluted, and animals are becoming extinct throughout the world at an alarming rate.

By setting up scientific preservation projects all over the world, many species can be saved through the acquisition of land, the protection of habitats, and the preservation of nature reserves. The WWF's long-range action plans bring together scientists, conservation groups, and other experts; together, they have been able to save or rescue from extinction the Arabian oryx, the peregrine falcon in America, and the Bengal tiger in India.

Defenders of Wildlife. Through education, litigation, research, and advocacy, Defenders of Wildlife has led the movement for the protection and preservation of wildlife habitats since 1947. It works primarily to inform Congress of the need for environmental protection, especially regarding the use of public lands, including land managed by the Department of the Interior. The work involves calling for less commercial development and more emphasis on preserving wildlands.

Defenders of Wildlife has effectively fought to eliminate the use of strychnine above the ground because it threatened the existence of fifteen already endangered species. The organization was also immediately on the scene at the Exxon oil spill in Alaska, analyzing its impact on the environment and reporting it to Congress. The group could be considered the private-sector watchdog of the federal agencies.

North American Wildlife Foundation. The mission of this group is to assist in the continuing efforts of effective, practical, and systematic research in local, national, and international management and techniques to benefit both wildlife and natural resources. The foundation accomplishes this through financial support, working through cooperating agencies and organizations. It also owns the Delta Waterfowl Research Station in Manitoba, Canada.

The Nature Conservancy. Established in 1951, the Nature Conservancy works to preserve biological diversity through land and water protection of natural areas. It identifies natural areas and then tries to protect those areas by buying them or working through cooperative management agreements with cooperating government or private agencies. It also supplies stewardship programs for sixteen hundred conservancy-owned areas and further protects them from destructive use.

A land acquisition begins when the conservancy identifies the environmental value of a certain piece of land—it contains rare prairie grass or is home to an endangered species, for example.

Once the land is acquired, the conservancy manages it for conservation or turns it over to other responsible agencies or educational facilities. So far, they have preserved more than five million acres in the United States and Canada. On these lands are animal sanctuaries, swamps, and wildlife habitats. The conservancy is an action-oriented organization that works to prevent the destruction of ecosystems and wildlife habitats and to stop the commercial takeover of public land before it happens.

Environmental Defense. This organization uses law, economics, science, and engineering to bring about creative solutions to environmental issues. It has four focus areas:

1. Protecting and restoring biodiversity
2. Stabilizing climate by developing policies to reduce dependency on fossil fuels
3. Reducing risks to human health from exposure to toxins
4. Protecting oceans from pollution and overfishing

Lawyers and scientists work together with economists to eliminate harmful pesticides, to protect porpoises from the tuna fishing industry, and to come up with alternatives to dumping plastics into the oceans.

The Wilderness Society. The mission of this organization is to establish a land ethic as a basic element of our culture and to educate a constituency to a more committed wilderness preservation and land protection ideal. Its focus is on federal, legislative, and administrative actions regarding public lands, including national parks and forests, refuges, and wilderness areas. Through grassroots organization, it emphasizes lobbying and research to achieve its goals.

The society has specifically targeted the U.S. Forest Service for its adverse logging policies. According to the society, the Forest

Service should be responsible for managing the forests in order to conserve wildlife habitat, preserve watersheds, and supply outdoor recreational facilities, as well as provide timber. The society believes that the Forest Service puts too much emphasis on selling timber quickly and cheaply, thereby undermining its conservation role.

International Wildlife Coalition. A global organization, the coalition seeks to preserve wildlife and habitats in the United States, Sri Lanka, Brazil, Australia, the United Kingdom, and Canada. It is affiliated with the Whale and Dolphin Conservation Society.

Whale and Dolphin Conservation Society. The society's Whale Adoption Project urges people to adopt humpback whales off the coast of Cape Cod. The adoption fee for a whale is used in the coalition's struggle against those countries that are still killing whales, even though the International Whaling Commission has declared a moratorium on whale kills. The adoptive whales are part of ongoing research and investigation by the Cetacean Research Program at the Provincetown Center for Coastal Studies. These researchers study behavioral patterns, reproduction, movement, and migratory activities of the whales.

Wildlife Conservation Society. The Wildlife Conservation Society operates the Bronx Zoo, the Aquarium for Wildlife Conservation, and three other wildlife centers in New York. It also maintains an office in Nairobi, Kenya. It conducts field studies, professional training sessions, and makes recommendations on conservation decisions. In the past twenty years, the African elephant population has declined by half. The society now is engaged in carefully monitoring elephant populations. It is also helping government agencies to acquire new land that will link up already existing parks and reserves, enabling elephants to roam more freely in their natural habitats.

African Wildlife Foundation. This foundation promotes programs that train Africans in wildlife management and ecology. It also offers technical assistance in park and resource management and provides equipment for antipoaching patrols.

International Association of Fish & Wildlife Agencies. Founded in 1902, this agency is charged with the mission of educating the public about the economic importance of preserving natural resources, managing wildlife property, and supporting better conservation legislation, administration, and enforcement.

Earth Island Institute. The institute is concerned with conservation on a global basis. It administers the International Marine Mammal Project, working to protect whales and dolphins by preventing their slaughter in tuna nets. One particular campaign targeted a major tuna packing company. After a major public awareness program, consumer boycotts, and many months of hard work, the institute obtained from the company a promise not to kill any more dolphins for tuna for any of their products, including pet food. It all started when an undercover biologist filmed the dolphins drowning in the tuna nets. The campaign then launched a massive public-information program, staged picket lines, sent thousands of Mailgrams to tuna companies, and made legal challenges in court and testified before government agencies. The institute is still trying to get other tuna companies to comply with the ban on dolphin kills. The goal is to achieve a total ban by all processing companies.

An Outreach Coordinator with a Private Conservation Organization

Sara Meghrouni is the outreach coordinator for the Save-the-Dolphins Project with the Earth Island Institute. She thinks that a strong grassroots organizational background is important for anyone who wants to work for a nonprofit organization involved in either habitat preservation or animal conservation. She thinks that people who were involved in campus activities or student organizations or clubs in school may be best suited to this work, since one gains in these activities the motivation to accept challenges and develop creativity. Working for a nonprofit organization requires an awareness of issues and legislative processes as well as office management skills.

Sara also recommends a business background, preferably with some fund-raising experience. Your undergraduate course work should be broadly based and could include law, anthropology, business administration, journalism, and science. Political awareness, involvement in campus activities, and working with other people will be every bit as valuable to you as your course work.

To work for the institute, you don't need a biology or zoology degree, although these would help if you wanted to work on research projects in the field or write for the institute's primary publication, the *Earth Island Journal*. If you are thinking of changing your career, you might consider volunteering at a wildlife conservation, environmental protection, or animal rights organization. Your exposure to the issues and the people involved will help you build contacts, and this networking is extremely important in nonprofit work.

Sara worked with animal rights groups and as a canvasser for Greenpeace before she got her job at Earth Island Institute. In addition to acquiring organizational skills in this position, she has also learned how to get the attention of the media, which is quite important in any nonprofit work. Media exposure is crucial in order to get your message across to the public.

Choosing Your Career in Wildlife Conservation and Management

Even if you are not physically working with the animals as a researcher, wildlife or aquatic biologist, or ornithologist, you can gain satisfaction in knowing that you are using your particular organizational, legal, journalistic, or administrative talents to work for the preservation of species, conservation of ecosystems, or restoration of wildlife habitats. You can do that either for a federal or state agency or in any one of the many nonprofit organizations dedicated to these purposes.

The choice between the public and private sectors is fairly clear-cut and entirely up to you. Government work may provide you with more stability and have more clearly defined requirements for education and eligibility. Since government jobs are funded through taxes, you would not need to be concerned with fundraising. But you would have to follow the policies of the particular administration in power, and those policies may include directives regarding land use, logging, habitat manipulation, and wildlife kills with which you disagree.

Nonprofit organizations are usually governed by a board of directors that sets policy for the group. But these nonprofit organizations are usually focused on a single issue or cluster of closely related issues. Therefore, when you work for an independent organization, you know exactly which cause you are working for. Among nonprofit organizations, there is probably be less emphasis on educational eligibility and more emphasis on commitment to philosophy and issues.

Whether your job is government or private, fieldwork or administrative, you will be working for the animals whose very existence may be in extreme jeopardy. Your job satisfaction should come from your knowledge that you have made a concrete contribution toward their survival.

. . . .

For More Information

Publications

Carlson, Dale Bick, and Irene Ruth. *Wildlife Care for Birds and Mammals: Basic Manuals Wildlife Rehabilitation.* Bick Publishing House, 1997.

The Humane Society of the United States: John Hadidian, Guy
R. Hodge, John W. Grandy, eds. *Wild Neighbors: The Humane
Approach to Living with Wildlife.* Fulcrum Publishing, 1997.

Schneck, Marcus H., and Jill Caravan. *Gorillas: A Portrait of the
Animal World.* New Line Books, 1999.

Wildlife Conservation Society. *State of the Wild: A Global Portrait
of Wildlife, Wildlands, and Oceans.* Island Press, 2005.

Associations

African Wildlife Foundation
1400 Sixteenth Street NW, Suite 120
Washington, DC 20036
www.awf.org

American Fisheries Society
5410 Grosvenor Lane, Suite 110
Bethesda, MD 20814
www.fisheries.org

American Institute of Biological Sciences
1441 I Street NW, Suite 200
Washington, DC 20005
www.aibs.org

Defenders of Wildlife
1130 Seventeenth Street NW
Washington, DC 20036
www.defenders.org

Earth Island Institute
300 Broadway, Suite 28
San Francisco, CA 94133
www.earthisland.org

Environmental Defense
257 Park Avenue South
New York, NY 10010
www.environmentaldefense.org

International Association of Fish & Wildlife Agencies
444 North Capitol Street NW, Suite 725
Washington, DC 20001
www.iafwa.org

International Wildlife Coalition
70 East Falmouth Highway
East Falmouth, MA 02536
www.iwc.org

The Nature Conservancy
4545 North Fairfax Drive, Suite 100
Arlington, VA 22203
www.nature.org

Sierra Club
85 Second Street, Second Floor
San Francisco, CA 94105
www.sierraclub.org

U.S. Department of the Interior
National Park Service
U.S. Fish and Wildlife Service
1849 C Street NW
Washington, DC 20240
www.doi.gov
www.fws.gov

Whale and Dolphin Conservation Society (North America)
70 East Falmouth Highway
East Falmouth, MA 02536
www.whales.org

The Wilderness Society
1615 M Street NW
Washington, DC 20036
www.wilderness.org

Wildlife Conservation Society
2300 Southern Boulevard
Bronx, NY 10460
www.wcs.org

Wildlife Management Institute
1146 Nineteenth Street NW, Suite 700
Washington, DC 20036
www.wildlifemanagementinstitute.org

The Wildlife Society
5410 Grosvenor Lane, Suite 200
Bethesda, MD 20814
www.wildlife.org

World Wildlife Fund
1250 Twenty-Fourth Street NW
Washington, DC 20090
www.worldwildlife.org

World Wildlife Fund–Canada
245 Eglinton Avenue East, Suite 410
Toronto, ON M4P 3J1
Canada
www.wwf.ca

CHAPTER NINE

Animal Welfare and Animal Rights Organizations

A growing number of organizations have sprung up in response to the need perceived by many to protect companion, farm, and wild animals. Large national organizations that focus on incremental improvements to conditions, usually with a particular focus on companion animals (dogs, cats, small pets, and horses) include the American Humane Association (AHA), the American Society for the Prevention of Cruelty to Animals (ASPCA, the oldest animal welfare organization in the country, founded in 1866 by Henry Bergh), and the Humane Society of the United States (HSUS, the largest animal welfare organization in the world), among others. The oldest of these organizations were modeled on similar organizations in Great Britain and were originally founded to do the work of both animal protection and the protection of children and women. Only one of these groups, the AHA, continues to pursue this double mandate.

Much of the work of these organizations is in support of local animal shelters and animal control organizations that work on the front lines in this arena. The national organizations often sponsor conferences and training seminars, publish materials, and provide some funding that helps local organizations keep up to state and national standards and improve beyond them. They also conduct public education efforts and work in the legislative arena, often with a focus on such topics as making sure families' disaster evacuation plans include the family pet, increasing penalties in cases of animal cruelty, and banning inhumane methods of animal euthanasia.

Other groups, known generally as animal rights organizations, are also often national organizations but focus on laboratory and classroom dissection, vivisection, factory farms, the slaughterhouse, fur farms, and various forms of inhumane treatment. Although these groups encounter much resistance from those who run the labs, farms, and slaughterhouses, they are finding an increasing number of supporters throughout the world.

The scope of their work is broad and ranges from encouraging the public to buy medications that are free of animal byproducts to providing alternatives to animal research. Or they may point out the danger of certain types of traps and nets or reveal how animals actually live on factory farms. These organizations may protest possible dangers to performing animals or urge the public to write members of Congress about a pending bill that would affect animals.

The common thread among their far-ranging efforts is the belief that humane living conditions should be provided to all species and that animal cruelty should be abolished. They believe that one species should never be protected by the destruction of another. Their aims generally include maintaining a deep commitment to the preservation of all species, including humans, through protecting the whole natural environment.

The practical efforts of such groups are generally oriented toward public education and action, with emphasis on educating the public and supporting legislation for the protection of animals. Many organizations focus on protecting a certain species or preventing a certain method of animal abuse. They launch campaigns that address the use of farm animals, performing animals, laboratory animals, animals in fur farms, racehorses, and racing dogs. They may also encourage a meatless lifestyle.

Although some groups occasionally go beyond their own specific interests and collaborate with environmental groups, each group is generally distinguished by its particular focus. Some organizations, though, are all-encompassing and take on problems affecting animal welfare as a whole.

Some organizations were started by medical caretakers, such as veterinarians, doctors, or psychologists; others were begun by a cross section of people of all social, occupational, and economic backgrounds. All are deeply concerned with the rights of animals.

The Animal Rights Movement

A major thrust for the animal rights movement came about with the publication of the book *Animal Liberation* by the Australian Peter Singer. Until then, there was little cohesion among those who opposed vivisection (animal experimentation) and those who opposed factory farming. The book encouraged many groups to focus and dialogue with each other. To many, the 1970s marked the beginning of the idea that all animals, including humans, have rights. The term *animal rights* began to appear in print. And people found out there was no effective legal protection for animals used in medical or corporate laboratories, farms, the entertainment industry, or circuses.

The budding environmental movement showed us how whole species were becoming endangered or extinct because of pollution and habitat destruction. Biologists realized that different species have different responses to drugs and, therefore, couldn't always be reliable for testing drugs meant eventually for humans. Computer technology became refined enough to be used to simulate experiments, and in vitro techniques made research on human tissues viable for detecting diseases.

Prevention Versus Cure

These years also produced scientists, doctors, and surgeons who were focusing more on the prevention of disease through clinical and epidemiological research than on surgical or medical cures developed through animal research. In fact, these professionals question the efficacy of animal research, noting that after many years of research on cancer, often with animals, we are no closer than before to a cure.

Clinical and epidemiological research often points to prevention, rather than cure, as the best means of treating disease. Lifestyle and diet are often shown to be the major contributing factors in the cause of some diseases, such as cancer, heart attack, and stroke. For example, the three main factors that seem to contribute to heart disease are high cholesterol, smoking, and high blood pressure. Alcohol consumption and pollution probably contribute to a lesser degree. Through effective preventive measures, these factors can be eliminated in our lifestyles, thus enabling us to avoid the more intrusive, more costly—and sometimes less effective—bypasses and transplants.

Epidemiological research has led many scientists to believe that some forms of cancer can be prevented through maintaining a low-fat diet, eliminating tobacco, increasing beta carotene in your diet, and decreasing exposure to the sun.

Epidemiological studies in the late 1970s also found the unusual symptoms of what turned out to be a major epidemic of our time—AIDS. Population studies demonstrated modes of transmission that led to ways of preventing infection.

Later, in vitro tests revealed what happens to the blood in human cells and tissues. Actually studying people with AIDS may identify the disease-fighting factors that characterize people who have successfully resisted the strain, without having to inject countless more animals with the disease. If successful, such a study could be a big step toward eliminating the syndrome.

Animal Research Alternatives

A related movement among medical researchers and scientists has been to replace experimental techniques using animals with nonanimal alternatives producing the same results. For example, the Ames Test, a nonanimal alternative testing procedure, has helped researchers determine whether certain substances cause genetic damage in salmonella bacteria. A synthetic copy of insulin, which has traditionally been taken from cows and pigs, is now widely available for diabetic patients. This synthetic, created through recombinant DNA technology, usually causes fewer allergic reactions than its animal-derived counterpart. In the field of oncology, a new method has been developed that tests potential drugs on the cells of human tumors. The results are then entered into a computer for analysis.

With all these advances in medical technology through nonanimal clinical tests, computer simulations, and epidemiological research, it is no wonder that the idea of using animals in the laboratories seemed outmoded and slow. And it is no wonder that the idea of animal rights in the laboratory grew from an isolated concept to a full-fledged movement by the 1980s and continues to this day.

With the animal rights movement's growth came resistance from corporations, medical schools, research facilities, and pharmaceutical firms that were the targets of the movement. Using animals in the laboratory and as part of medical training had become ingrained and was difficult to change.

Farming Reform

Many activists date the need for the animal rights movement even earlier, to the 1960s, when people began to see a change in farming methods. Before that, most farms were owned by families who had, in many cases, owned their farms for generations. Chickens, pigs, and cows, even though they were bred for slaughter, freely roamed the farmland before being killed. Farmers personally fed the animals, saw to their health, and milked the cows by hand or machine. The animals were allowed to lead a natural social life, and the mothers were allowed to stay with their young for an appropriate time and bear a normal number of young per year.

With the population explosion, however, there was a need to feed more and more people more quickly. Many fast-food franchises and chain supermarkets sprang up, needing cheap beef and chicken to supply daily to millions of people. In order to supply these proliferating franchises with enough meat, the whole farming business changed.

Huge factory farms were developed to raise more animals destined for human consumption. In such places, according to animal protection groups, four to five laying hens are crammed into one-foot-square wire cages for their entire lives. Male chicks are suffocated, drowned, or crushed to death, and females have their beaks seared off to prevent them from pecking each other to death.

Veal calves, taken from their mothers at birth, are chained to small pens where they cannot stand up or move and are kept on a synthetic diet that keeps their flesh white. This vitamin-deficient food is usually laced with antibiotics in an often unsuccessful attempt to prevent disease. These antibiotics may, ironically, increase human susceptibility to infectious diseases.

Some people claim that modern factory farming, combined with farm subsidy programs, has led to the overproduction of cattle and chickens and even to the destruction of rain forests. Others say that affluent consumers' need for milk-fed veal has led to the substandard living conditions of veal calves. Still others blame the emphasis placed on milk consumption in adult humans for the fact that calves are deprived of their own mothers' milk.

Whatever the issue, the protest against factory farms and for more humane treatment of farm animals is growing and getting more publicity in the process. Organizations formed and placed ads in newspapers, magazines, and public transportation systems. These groups actively work against the caged lives of veal calves, breeding sows, and laying hens and against the health effects of the bovine growth hormone on the health of dairy cows. Some groups encourage a meatless lifestyle, since there is some evidence that the consumption of animal fat leads to heart disease, cancer, and stroke.

Working for Animal Rights Organizations

There are many organizations working hard to introduce and change laws, to educate the public, and to change traditional methods of using and thinking about animals. Needless to say, they will remain controversial and outside the mainstream. But a career with such an organization will never be dull. It will, however, require a deep commitment, a thorough knowledge of the facts regarding the issues, and a great deal of perseverance.

Animal Rights Organizations in Operation

Let's take a look at some of these groups and see whether they offer the kind of work that you would be interested in. Because there are so many, and since they all have different focuses, you may find one that matches your interests exactly.

Physicians Committee for Responsible Medicine. Located in Washington, D.C., the Physicians Committee for Responsible Medicine (PCRM) works for animal welfare in a variety of ways. The group provides education programs in human nutrition and health; encourages the prevention of disease through healthy lifestyle and diet rather than animal experimentation; and campaigns against the use of live animals in medical school curricula.

PCRM objects strongly to the use of thousands of animals in government-funded studies that feed monkeys ethanol to the point that they develop irreversible liver damage; inject monkeys and baboons with MDMA, commonly known as ecstasy, causing brain damage and death; and kill and dissect cats after injecting them with methamphetamine and with feline HIV.

Millions of animals are burned, blinded, stressed, or injected before they are killed in the United States. PCRM's stance is that these are completely useless experiments that are paid for through our taxes. Many of these experiments test an animal's reactions to drug- or alcohol-related effects and stress that apply only to humans.

For example, MRIs of affected patients can better assess the human nervous system and its relationship to stress in humans with addiction problems. Interviewing addicts and their relatives has also been found to be an effective form of assessing factors involved in substance abuse. The best way, in other words, to get to the root cause of stress and addiction, PCRM argues, is by studying the factors that affect human life, not through the cruel and inhumane use of animals.

Society & Animals Forum. The Society & Animals Forum (formerly Psychologists for the Ethical Treatment of Animals) was founded in 1981 and is concerned with the suffering of animals in research and educational facilities, in training, on the farm, and in performance. It has expanded its original mission to reduce suffering, violence, and exploitation in human and nonhuman animals. It achieves its goals through workshops, publications, manuals, and advocacy programs.

Humane Farming Association. A few independent organizations specialize in farm animal protection issues. The Humane Farming Association has launched campaigns against factory farming in general and treatment of veal calves in particular. The group approaches its work from more than one angle: education of the public, boycotts of the producers, legal action, and legislation. Its mission also extends to protecting the public from the hazards of antibiotics, hormones, and other chemicals used in factory farming.

Farm Animal Reform Movement. The Farm Animal Reform Movement conducts campaigns on a variety of issues, although the veal issue is one of primary importance. The movement promotes a plant-based diet and works for the elimination of farm-animal abuse and other inhumane impacts on animals in agriculture.

The movement, founded in 1981, originated because of a growing awareness of intensive animal agriculture, often called agribusiness. The movement operates through a network of local groups and individuals in the United States and Canada.

The group instigated a campaign to ban veal, which was effective in persuading restaurants not to serve veal. It also staged a sit-in at the office of the Secretary of Agriculture and conducted slaughterhouse vigils and a compassion campaign.

The movement is opposed to immobilizing sows in cages and keeping them continuously pregnant; to keeping laying hens in battery cages where they are debeaked to prevent cannibalism; to resource destruction caused by raising so many animals for food; and to the use of antibiotics in animal feed.

The movement also promotes a vegetarian lifestyle, and toward that end it conducts the annual Great American Meatout, which reaches about twenty million people through a variety of events. It also sponsors the World Farm Animals Day, which features exhibits, marches, memorials, and civil disobedience.

The organization has also developed a humane farming curriculum for high school students and advanced skills seminars for activists. It is developing a farm animal humane education module for school curricula that will consist of illustrated fact sheets describing the factory farm and offering suggestions to improve it.

Animal Protection Institute of America. The Animal Protection Institute of America also sees a threat to farm animals. This group was started in 1968 and boasts a membership of 150,000, with 10,000 special volunteers. It is concerned with farm animals, as well as with wildlife and habitat, legislation affecting animals, and all threats to animal life.

Animal Legal Defense Fund. The Animal Legal Defense Fund (ALDF) was started in 1979 when a group of lawyers decided that they wanted to learn about legislation protecting animals. The animal rights movement was growing, but there was no national organization that provided legal expertise on vital issues regarding animal welfare. Today the group functions as the sole nationwide legal organization dedicated to the promotion and defense of animal rights. It defends the rights of wildlife, farm animals, and companion animals in the home, on the farm, in the laboratory, and in the wild.

The fund works to give a voice to innocent animal victims of mistreatment, cruelty, or abuse. The group's more than forty-five thousand members use a network of more than three hundred lawyers and law students to fight for the welfare of animals in the courts and in Congress. The group created an Animal Bill of Rights to send to the 101st Congress. It takes legal action against any government entities, corporations, educational, and research facilities that are in violation of the Animal Welfare Act of 1966 or the Federal Law Enforcement Animal Protection Act of 2000. It has halted deer and black bear hunts in Illinois and California, for example.

Members call ALDF the "the law firm of the animal rights movement." Their issues may concern animal patenting, wildlife protection, consumer products testing, or genetic manipulation. ALDF maintains a list of attorneys available for legal assistance and is prepared to give students advice on negotiating with school officials or teachers against dissection or even to provide legal assistance.

ALDF recently released a ranking of state animal protection laws because so many of them are weak and provide no substantial protection for animals or punishment for abusers. In some states, for example, animal cruelty is a felony, subject to possible jail time and/or a substantial fine, while in others, abusers may only be convicted of a misdemeanor with no jail time or fine.

ALDF seeks to strengthen the weaker laws to help deter animal cruelty.

People for the Ethical Treatment of Animals. People for the Ethical Treatment of Animals (PETA) claims to be the largest animal rights organization in the world. It defends all animals in all circumstances. Its concerns encompass factory farm animals, fur farm animals, entertainment or performing animals, and laboratory animals. PETA's goal is to relieve pain and suffering of all these animals. Its members launch campaigns to publicize the results of their investigations and research; they stage demonstrations against toy manufacturers, corporations, and government agencies; they call for boycotts of animal-tested products and animals in entertainment; they encourage letter-writing campaigns to Congress on pending legislation; they investigate, publicize, and file lawsuits to further the organization's goals.

PETA's publications inform members of the latest campaigns and pending laws, provide meatless recipes and nutritional advice, supply activities for children, and feature pertinent follow-up on ongoing campaigns. The organization also publishes a catalog offering books, videos, and gift ideas.

National Anti-Vivisection Society. The main purpose of the National Anti-Vivisection Society (NAVS) is educating the public about the cruelty of using animals in research or medical testing and training. The group performs its work by holding classes, disseminating literature, lecturing, and forming new antivivisection societies where needed. One of its major efforts has been the campaign waged against Lethal Dose-50 (LD-50), which is the amount of a substance that will kill half of a test group of animals within a specified time, and the Draize Test, which attempts to measure the harmfulness of chemicals to humans by testing them on the eyes and skin of animals. Making known the alternatives to animal testing and encouraging the use of cosmetics and cleaning products that do not use animals for experimentation was the chief goal of this campaign.

NAVS also sponsors lectures by proponents of humane treatment of animals, reports on technological advances and pending legislation that will affect animals, and introduces members to new organizations or to new projects sponsored by existing organizations.

Through its quarterly *Bulletin*, NAVS prints pertinent articles, publicizes new books, and encourages letter-writing campaigns against offending corporations or to members of Congress who are on committees concerning animal welfare legislation. The society also publishes a catalog of cruelty-free products for its members called *Personal Care for People Who Care*.

NAVS has also established The NAVS Sanctuary Fund, which provides emergency assistance to animals who are victims of natural or manmade disasters and for those who have recently been retired from research. The fund provides lifelong care for these animals by reaching out to worthy organizations that need emergency grants.

In Defense of Animals. A similar organization, In Defense of Animals (IDA), was started by a veterinarian to protest the LD-50 and Draize tests, animal addiction experiments, and the use of fur and ivory.

Headquartered in San Rafael, California, the group claims to have fifty thousand members and supporters who are encouraged to boycott specific corporations that still use research animals in their laboratories and to protest against any corporate or educational organization that conducts animal experimentations.

In addition to these causes, IDA has launched a campaign against the cruel treatment of dogs and cats in South Korea that are victims of the meat trade there. The animals die a long, drawn-out, painful death in the mistaken belief that the longer it takes to kill the animal, the better it will taste.

Animal Welfare Institute. The Animal Welfare Institute has as its primary goal the elimination of cruel trapping of animals and of the destruction of whales and other endangered species. In addition, it works against the use of exotic birds for commercial use and against cruelty to animals used for food and for experiments and testing.

Animal Rights International. This organization unites individuals and organizations to reduce the use of animals in testing, research, and education while not endangering humans. It encourages the use of substitute tests that do not require animals at all or that use fewer animals and reduce their pain and suffering.

Equine Advocate. Established in 1996, this organization is actively opposed to the practice of slaughtering horses in the United States, where many people consider them to be companion animals rather than food, for export to European and Japanese food markets. Equine Advocates claims that millions of American horses have been brutally slaughtered in the United States and in Canada, and that one hundred thousand horses are slaughtered for consumption abroad every year. Equine Advocates works through educating the public, investigating abuses, and conducting rescue operations.

Return to Freedom. Return to Freedom is a wild horse sanctuary seeking to save the wild horse population in the United States. It was founded as a response to Montana's Senator Conrad Burns who, without public debate, condemned thousands of wild horses to slaughter in the context of a huge funding bill. Removing the horses from public lands is done at great expense to U.S. taxpayers, estimated at $30 million annually, when there is no overpopulation of wild horses. Often, these horses are slaughtered and then exported to various European and Asian countries and sold for food.

Association of Veterinarians for Animal Rights. The Association of Veterinarians for Animal Rights in Vacaville, California, was founded by veterinarians who decided to apply their scientific knowledge to the elimination of animal suffering in medical and product research. Its members are doing this through a national education program that involves television and radio spots and ads in newspapers and magazines. They do not confine membership in the organization to veterinarians.

Its members have also testified whenever possible at public hearings on legislation affecting animal welfare. They are also starting student chapters at veterinary schools throughout the country and hope to reach all schools with preveterinary programs in the near future.

These veterinarians are also against turning impounded animals over for use in research. They favor using nonanimal alternatives in research, such as computer simulations and tissue culture. In veterinary schools, they favor the use of inanimate objects in order to practice manual dexterity and the use of animal cadavers for advanced procedures. During clinical training, they encourage using actual animal patients only on the most basic operations. They also oppose the housing of veal calves in crates and believe that if veal calves must be raised for slaughter, they should at least be housed more humanely and thus enabled to live normal (though abbreviated) lives.

Employment Opportunities in Animal Rights Organizations

We have looked at a cross section of animal protective organizations so that you can make a well-informed career choice. These nonprofit organizations often operate on limited budgets. Some groups may receive grants or endowments; others may be completely dependent on membership donations. You may need to be willing to live very modestly if you are employed by a nonprofit organization.

Animal protection agencies are headquartered throughout the country, so you may have to relocate in order to work for them. Some organizations are headed by and do the work of veterinarians, psychologists, or legal specialists; others include more broadly based occupations. Most rely on a large group of volunteers.

As with many other jobs that are focused on animal care and welfare, you may want to volunteer with one of these organizations before actually applying for employment. Volunteering for a local chapter or branch in your area would help you to decide whether you want to be employed by that organization before you relocate.

Some organizations have a well-established structure, with a board of directors, chief executive officer, and other officers, including vice presidents, secretaries, and treasurers. Other groups may be more flexible, but administration will always have certain responsibilities, such as setting policy and procedures and hiring and training personnel.

Many other possibilities for employment exist in the field of animal rights law. Since more and more laws are pending that affect the rights of animals, lawyers will be needed to testify at public hearings, litigate on behalf of animals' rights, and advise animal rights organizations.

The public's growing awareness of the factory farming system will create a need for farm animal behaviorists to work toward more humane treatment of all farm animals, including pigs, cows, veal calves, cattle, and poultry.

Veterinarians will be needed to teach in educational facilities to encourage alternatives to animal use in laboratories and in surgical procedures. Psychologists will be needed to examine and alter public attitudes toward animals.

The field of alternatives to animals in research is rapidly growing because of new technologies and the use of human cells in epidemiological studies to investigate the causes of human diseases.

Some animal protection organizations maintain shelters for rescued animals or wildlife preserves. These need wildlife biologists and behaviorists and often wildlife refuge managers.

People with journalism backgrounds are also needed because of their writing abilities and knowledge of the media. Most animal rights organizations need people who know how to write press releases and who have contacts with the working press to help publicize the organization's work. Investigators and researchers are always needed in animal rights work, in addition to animal advocates.

Many of these organizations have grown from grassroots movements, and no particular education or training in animal work is necessary for employment. Organizational and communications skills and a deep commitment to the cause are helpful, though, and reliability, dependability, and willingness to work long hours are also valuable qualifications.

An increasing number of people who work for national advocacy organizations—as well as for local shelters and refuges—have earned master's degrees from the Center for Animals and Public Policy at Tufts University in Massachusetts or from one of several similar programs offered around the country. In these programs, students take an in-depth look at overarching issues such as pet overpopulation and what causes the breakdown of the human-animal bond. They learn how to design and conduct studies that may lead to the next breakthroughs in these areas.

For professional occupations, such as physician, veterinarian, psychologist, lawyer, and teacher, you will, of course, need specialized education and training. The same applies to biologists, ornithologists, and aquarists.

As society changes, as technology advances, as new laws are passed or rescinded, new organizations will be founded and new people will be needed for the work. Since these organizations are fairly new in the field of animal work, the prospects for the future are quite good.

The work on alternatives to animals, the possibilities for developing products without animal experimentation, the increasing use of human cells for research, and the refusal of many veterinary students to operate on live, healthy animals for experimentation—all of these mean new employment opportunities for professionals and nonprofessionals alike. Researchers who are trained in preventive medicine and humane research techniques should be in great demand.

The American Bar Association now has an Animal Protection Committee, which publishes the newsletter *Animal Law Report*. With the Animal Bill of Rights, even more possibilities may open up for those who work on the legal side of animal work. This bill of rights basically guarantees that animals will remain free of cruel treatment and exploitation, that farm animals are granted basic needs, and that wildlife is entitled to a natural habitat, among other items.

With more and more emphasis being placed on the survival of the total environment through the preservation of whole ecological systems, the plight of animals will be increasingly publicized, and more people will be needed than ever before to work toward solving these myriad problems. You might be one of them.

If you are interested in a career with one of these organizations, contact the one you feel suits you best and find out whether your talents and skills could be utilized. Or you may see a need currently unaddressed and decide to found your own group. You need to become aware of what is being done on behalf of animals and what still needs to be accomplished. This may entail a great deal of preliminary reading, becoming a member of an organization that does the work you're interested in, and performing volunteer work for that organization.

. . . .

For More Information

Publications

Rudacille, Deborah. *The Scalpel and the Butterfly: The War Between Animal Research and Animal Protection.* Farrar, Straus and Giroux, 2000.

Scully, Matthew. *Dominion: The Power of Man, the Suffering of Animals, and the Call to Mercy.* St. Martin's Griffin, 2003.

Wise, Steven M. *Rattling the Cage: Toward Legal Rights for Animals.* Perseus Publishing, 2000.

Associations

American Humane Association (AHA)
63 Inverness Drive East
Englewood, CO 80112
www.americanhumane.org

American Society for the Prevention of Cruelty to Animals (ASPCA)
424 East Ninety-Second Street
New York, NY 10128
www.aspca.org

Animal Legal Defense Fund
170 East Cotati Avenue
Cotati, CA 94931
www.aldf.org

Animal Protection Institute of America
PO Box 22505
Sacramento, CA 95822
www.api4animals.org

Animal Rights Coalition
PO Box 8750
Minneapolis, MN 55408
www.animalrightscoalition.com

Animal Rights International
PO Box 532
Woodbury, CT 06798
www.ari-online.org

Animal Welfare Institute
PO Box 3650
Georgetown Station
Washington, DC 20027
www.awionline.org

Association of Veterinarians for Animal Rights
PO Box 208
Davis, CA 95617
www.avar.org

Equine Advocates
PO Box 354
Chatham, NY 12037
www.equineadvocates.com

Farm Animal Reform Movement
10101 Ashburton
Bethesda, MD 20817
www.farmusa.org

Humane Farming Association
PO Box 3577
San Rafael, CA 94912
www.hfa.org

The Humane Society of the United States (HSUS)
2100 L Street NW
Washington, DC 20037
www.hsus.org

In Defense of Animals
3010 Kerner Boulevard
San Rafael, CA 94901
www.idausa.org

Institute for Animal Rights Law
www.instituteforanimalrightslaw.org

Johns Hopkins University Center for Alternatives
    to Animal Testing
111 Market Place, Suite 840
Baltimore, MD 21202
http://caat.jhsph.edu

National Anti-Vivisection Society
53 West Jackson Boulevard, Suite 1552
Chicago, IL 60604
www.navs.org

People for the Ethical Treatment of Animals (PETA)
501 Front Street
Norfolk, VA 23510
www.peta.org

Physicians Committee for Responsible Medicine
5100 Wisconsin Avenue NW, Suite 400
Washington, DC 20016
www.pcrm.org

Return to Freedom
PO Box 926
Lompoc, CA 93438
www.returntofreedom.org

Society & Animals Forum (formerly Psychologists for the
 Ethical Treatment of Animals)
PO Box 1297
Washington Grove, MD 20880
www.psyeta.org

Center for Animals and Public Policy
Tufts University
200 Westboro Road
North Grafton, MA 01536
www.tufts.edu/vet/cfa

About the Author

....

Louise Miller has been an animal lover since she was first introduced to the family dog, Sugar, and the wonder of cats with Susie. Her respect for animals and their incredible contributions to our lives has been extended to other species, both wild and domesticated. In addition to animals, Miller loves languages, especially English and German. She started out as a German teacher in various colleges and universities and continues to tutor today. She has studied in Vienna, Austria, and Bonn, Germany.

Her love of English led her to teaching, writing, editing, and proofreading. She has taught English at community and business colleges, has conducted writing workshops, and has worked both full-time and freelance for a variety of publishing houses. These include Compton's Encyclopedia, Rand McNally & Company, World Book, and School Zone.

Other books Miller has written in this series are *Careers for Nature Lovers & Other Outdoor Types* and *Careers for Night Owls & Other Insomniacs*. Children's books include *VGM's Career Portraits: Animals* and *Turkey: Between East and West*. Miller is also a contributing writer for Rand McNally's book *America*. She is currently marketing and communications manager for a nonprofit organization.